HAYDN

SOLO PIANO LITERATURE

A Comprehensive Guide:

Annotated
and
Evaluated
with
Thematics

Edited by
Carolyn Maxwell

Assistant Editor
Charles Shadle

MAXWELL
MUSIC
EVALUATION

ACKNOWLEDGMENTS

Charles Shadle—Foreword and Prefaces
Elizabeth Harris—Cover Design
Kenneth Andrus—Production

Contributors
Christine Armstrong
William DeVan
Eileen Emerson
Marti Epstein
Mary Mosher Humm
Gayle Kliever
Steven Laitz
Charles Shadle

Published by Maxwell Music Evaluation Books
1245 Kalmia, Boulder, Colorado 80302

First printing, 1983

Printed in the United States of America.

ISBN 0-912531-00-2

TABLE OF CONTENTS

FOREWORD

Universally esteemed as one of the most important and influential composers of the classical era, Franz Joseph Haydn (1732-1809) is, in many respects, unknown as a creator of solo keyboard music. Until quite recently, both popular and critical opinion relegated a large percentage of the music of the galant and early classical periods to virtual obscurity. The earlier keyboard works of Haydn have fallen victim to this common prejudice regarding the supposed superficial crudity of these styles. Just criticism has often been leveled against the piano works of Haydn because of the admitted inconsistency of quality. Certainly the element of continual inspiration is less apparent in the keyboard music than in the string quartets and symphonies, yet considering the constant demands on Haydn's time and musical imagination, occasional lapses in quality are understandable. Much of Haydn's work, like that of his contemporaries, is expendable music, composed to order for specific occasions. However, many of the piano works reveal the consummate mastery and profound expressivity of the mature Haydn—characteristics which mark him as the most significant and representative composer of his generation. Finally, the voluminous body of work associated with Haydn, and especially the lack of an authoritative and complete scholarly edition of this music has hindered realization of the magnitude of Haydn's achievement in this medium. HAYDN: Solo Piano Literature is an attempt to fill the need for a practical and functional basic survey of the composer's keyboard compositions. This volume, with its logical format and concise, informative text, is accessible to musicians of a wide range of ages, abilities, and interests.

HAYDN: Solo Piano Literature is divided into six chapters which correspond to the basic categories encountered in the corpus of piano compositions associated with Haydn. Chapters I and II include all of the works originally conceived for klavier. All the arrangements of other compositions personally transcribed by Haydn are contained in Chapter III. The pieces for musical clock, Chapter VI, complete the canon of authentic keyboard works. Chapter IV includes versions of well-known Haydn works by a number of generally anonymous transcribers, and the pieces in Chapter V are compositions often associated with the master, yet their origins are in question.

Within each chapter, organization is based on the pioneering cataloguing system of Anthony van Hoboken, first published in Joseph Haydn Thematisch - bibliographische Werkverzeichnis. Although this invaluable publication is no longer complete or truly accurate, it provides a useful framework on which to base a survey of Haydn's piano works. Consequently, chapters are ordered according to the Hoboken (Hob.) catalogue whenever possible, and where a composition lacks this identifying number, it has been grouped by genre and key. As the Hoboken chronology is now inadequate, dates and approximate dates, based on contemporary research, are provided.

Each review within the chapter is divided into several component parts. The critiques begin with the title of the work, its key, level of difficulty, Hoboken catalogue number, date (where available), and in the case of the transcriptions, a reference to the original version of the piece. A thematic example extracted from the work follows, as does a comprehensive listing of currently available publications of the work. Individual sources are not given for the sonatas, as these works are quite readily available. A discussion of the piece is then presented, which comments on the salient formal and technical features and provides a critical evaluation of the work, respective of musical quality and pedagogical and performance values. The subjective viewpoint expressed in each commentary reflects a synthesis of the opinions of a number of highly qualified scholars and musicians. A summary of tempo, length, and notable technical features concludes each review.

Two indexes as well as a chart clarifying the divergent numbering systems of the sonatas have been appended. Measure numbers refer only to the number of printed bars: repeats and da capos have been omitted, while the second endings are included. Only those compositions associated with Haydn that are found in modern, accessible editions have been reviewed. However, as a convenience to the reader, thematics have been published for the seven lost sonatas, and for authentic transcriptions that are not readily available. HAYDN: Solo Piano Literature is a useful reference guide for anyone interested in the keyboard music of Haydn.

I. AUTHENTIC PIECES

Although Haydn's most significant contribution to the pianist's repertoire lies in the direction of the solo sonata, the body of larger independent compositions contains a number of characteristic works. These pieces are primarily patterned on variation and rondo forms, as these genres were the principle mode of structural expression for the isolated extended keyboard work in the eighteenth century. Both forms tended toward a style in which obvious clarity and structural repetition were combined with a diverting, perhaps superficial character. These works provided the vehicle of musical entertainment so conspicuous in the social climate of an era that emphasized grace and mannered affability. The more demanding dialectic of the fully developed sonata/allegro was reserved for musical matters of greater depth and import. Divorced from their role in the eighteenth century cultural milieu, these compositions may appear dated and trivial, though the works quite adequately represent an important aesthetic tenet of the age. All the major composers of the period regularly produced "light music" specifically intended as amiable badinage for the cultivated salon.

Haydn composed a number of works solely as elegant divertimenti, and the Variations Hob. XVII:2, Hob. XVII:5, and the possibly spurious Hob. XVII:7 belong to this category. These variations are characterized by simple, harmonically straightforward tunes, elaborate figuration which closely follows the melodic patterns, and brilliant virtuosity. Wit and joviality are apparent, yet they reveal little of Haydn's penetrating structural and harmonic inventiveness.

However, some of Haydn's single movement piano works are indelibly impressed with the stamp of the composer's particular genius. The attractive, if little known, Variations Hob. XVII:3 are harmonically resourceful as is the splendid set in F Minor. These Variations Hob. XVII:6, originally entitled "Sonata" by the composer, are among Haydn's greatest works. An elaborate and expressive double theme is subjected to two extensive variation sections and supplied with a brilliant and effective coda. Consistently intriguing harmonically and structurally, these variations are a profoundly beautiful testament to the vitality and inventiveness of the composer's mature style. The earlier Capriccio is garrulous, but boisterous and energetic, and quite delightful in its galant playfulness. Equally animated and exuberant, the harmonically venturesome Fantasia is a more rigorously structured work whose rondo-like format is pervaded by an elemental joy. Mention should be made of an Adagio Hob. XVII:9, a pleasant trifle which is perhaps a transcription by the composer of a now lost instrumental work. Another Adagio is occasionally listed in the canon of Haydn's solo piano works, but it is in fact an earlier version of the slow movement of the Sonata in C Major Hob. XVI:50. The independent piano works of Haydn are a microcosm of the composer's creative achievement: unassuming, less structurally secure pieces intended only to titillate the rococo sensibility, coexist with powerfully classical designs of vast expressive scope.

CAPRICCIO, G Major,   Advancing Intermediate
    Hob.XVII:1 (1765)

FERGUSON, Howard: Style and Interpretation, Vol. 3.
    (Oxford).
GERLACH, Sonja: Haydn Klavierstücke--Urtext
    (G. Henle Verlag).
HANSEN (Publisher): Joseph Haydn--A Highlight
    Collection...
KALMUS, #3534: Haydn--Eight Various Compositions
    (Belwin-Mills).

PHILIPP, Isadore: J. Haydn--Huit Pieces
(Durand No. 11592).
SHEALY, Alexander: Haydn--His Greatest Piano Solos
(Ashley).
SOLDAN, Kurt: Haydn--Klavierstücke --Urtext
(Peters Nr. 4392).

One of Haydn's major works for keyboard, this
Capriccio may be compared to any of the sonata movements for compositional quality. Although very long, it
is unified by a modified rondo form. The main thematic
material derives from the folksong Acht Sauschneider
müssen sein. The piece is recommended for
performance purposes as it is interesting for both the
pianist and the listener.

> Tempo: Moderato
> Length: 368 measures
> Technique: scales, arpeggios, trills, broken
>   octaves, sustained and moving notes,
>   double notes, Alberti bass, ornaments

ARIETTA WITH 19 VARIATIONS, A Major,   <u>Advanced</u>
Hob.XVII:2 (1765)

GERLACH, Sonja: Haydn Klavierstücke--Urtext
(G. Henle Verlag) 20 variations.
HANSEN (Publisher): Joseph Haydn--A Highlight
Collection...19 variations.
KALMUS #3534: Haydn--Eight Various Compositions
(Belwin-Mills) 18 variations.
PHILIPP, Isadore: J. Haydn--Huit Pieces
(Durand No. 11592) 18 variations.
SHEALY, Alexander: Haydn--His Greatest Piano Solos
(Ashley) 18 variations.

SOLDAN, Kurt: Joseph Haydn--Klavierstücke--Urtext
(Peters Nr. 4392) 19 variations.

Musically, this set of variations has a rococo
charm. The theme is pleasant sounding and many of the
variations are lovely, though some are less interesting. The piece provides pure tactile pleasure as it
contains many virtuosic passages. This work could be
performed in its entirety or with selected variations.
The easy Arietta theme is often published separately.

> Tempo: Allegretto
> Length: 320 measures (336 in Gerlach edition)
> Technique: scales, arpeggios, double notes,
>   sustained and moving notes, trills, octaves,
>   octave leaps, 2 against 3, crossed hands,
>   finger facility

ARIETTA WITH 12 VARIATIONS, Eb Major,   Advanced
Hob.XVII:3 (1770-1774)

GERLACH, Sonja: Haydn Klavierstücke--Urtext
(G. Henle Verlag).
HANSEN (Publisher): Joseph Haydn--A Highlight
Collection...
KALMUS #3534: Haydn--Eight Various Compositions
(Belwin-Mills).
PHILIPP, Isadore: J. Haydn--Huit Pieces
(Durand No. 11592).
SHEALY, Alexander: Haydn--His Greatest Piano Solos
(Ashley) 11 variations.
SOLDAN, Kurt: Haydn--Klavierstücke--Urtext
(Peters Nr. 4392).

This set of variations is one of Haydn's most beautiful and absorbing, containing numerous compositional

and pianistic effects, unusual harmonies, and expressive articulations. Voicing is important throughout. Accompanimental figures should be subdued to allow the simple nature of the theme to be heard. The Henle Urtext is recommended, since there are many discrepancies in dynamics, articulations, phrasings, and ornamentations among other editions. Variations feature fast scales, ornamentation, dotted rhythms, and a full spectrum of developmental devices. Many variations require careful voicing of the inner lines. This successful performance piece is geared to the pianist with well developed technique.

> Tempo: Moderato
> Length: 260 measures
> Technique: scales, arpeggios, trills,
>   ornaments, broken octaves, sustained and
>   moving notes, double notes

FANTASIA, C Major, Hob.XVII:4 (1789)   <u>Advanced</u>

FERGUSON, Howard: Oxford Keyboard Classics--Haydn
    (Oxford).
GERLACH, Sonja: Haydn Klavierstücke--Urtext
    (G. Henle Verlag).
HANSEN (Publisher): Joseph Haydn--A Highlight
    Collection...
HEINRICHSHOFEN (Publisher): Haydn--Easier
    Favorites, Urtext (Peters #4049).
KALMUS #3534: Haydn--Eight Various Compositions
    (Belwin-Mills).
PHILIPP, Isadore: J. Haydn--Huit Pieces
    (Durand No. 11592).
SHEALY, Alexander: Haydn--His Greatest Piano Solos
    (Ashley).

SOLDAN, Kurt: Haydn--Klavierstücke--Urtext
(Peters Nr. 4392).

The Fantasia is good-natured and highly recommended for playing enjoyment and performance. It is actually a rondo, made up of a free-form group of sections organized by a light-hearted theme. Haydn is harmonically very daring in this piece, modulating to a number of distantly related keys. Though full of "fantasia-like" characteristics such as cadenzas and other virtuosic passages, this work is not too difficult.
> Tempo: Presto
> Length: 467 measures
> Technique: arpeggios, trills, double notes,
>   scales, sustained and moving notes, octave
>   leaps, complex rhythms

VARIATIONS, C Major,   Advancing Intermediate
    Hob.XVII:5 (1789) (Six Variations)

ALFRED (Publisher): Haydn--15 of his Most Popular...
GERLACH, Sonja: Haydn Klavierstücke--Urtext
    (G. Henle Verlag).
HANSEN (Publisher): Joseph Haydn--A Highlight
    Collection...
HEINRICHSHOFEN (Publisher): Haydn--Easier
    Favorites, Urtext (Peters #4049).
HUGHES, Edwin: Haydn--Master Series for the Young
    (G. Schirmer).
KALMUS #3534: Haydn--Eight Various Compositions
    (Belwin-Mills).
PHILIPP, Isadore: J. Haydn--Huit Pieces
    (Durand No. 11592).
SHEALY, Alexander: Haydn--His Greatest Piano Solos
    (Ashley).

SOLDAN, Kurt: Haydn—Klavierstücke--Urtext
(Peters Nr. 4392).

Complex rhythms constitute the major difficulty in
this theme and variations, which is particularly successful because of the mood changes between sections.
It requires both musicality and finger facility. Short
enough to play in its entirety, it is an excellent recital
or audition piece. The brilliant ending is exciting for
both audience and performer.

> Tempo: Andante
> Length: 115 measures
> Technique: scales, fast runs, Alberti bass,
> arpeggios, double notes, complex rhythms

VARIATIONS, F Minor, Hob.XVII:6 (1793)   Advanced
(Un Piccolo Divertimento)

AGAY, Denes: Classics to Moderns, Themes and
  Variations, Vol. 77 (Consolidated).
FERGUSON, Howard: Oxford Keyboard Classics--Haydn
  (Oxford).
GERLACH, Sonja: Haydn Klavierstücke--Urtext
  (G. Henle Verlag).
HANSEN (Publisher): Joseph Haydn--A Highlight
  Collection...
KALMUS #3534: Haydn--Eight Various Compositions
  (Belwin-Mills).
PHILIPP, Isadore: J. Haydn--Huit Pieces
  (Durand No. 11592).
SOLDAN, Kurt: Haydn--Klavierstücke--Urtext
  (Peters Nr. 4392).

Among the greatest masterworks of Haydn's later
years, the Variations Hob.XVII:6 is particularly note-

worthy.   An exquisitely balanced double theme is
followed by two elaborate variations and a coda rich in
virtuosic elements.   The two-part theme (one of the
longest in the classical repertoire) ensures continual
structural diversity.   The formal achievement of the
work is complemented by a poignant and elegant harmonic sense, providing the basis for one of Haydn's most
stunning designs.   The technical demands, such as hand-
crossing and expressive clarity of voicing, are easily
overcome by a mature pianist.   Long regarded as the
apex of Haydn's piano music, these variations remain
perennially fresh and are a delighftul addition to any
recital or audition program.

   Tempo: Andante
   Length: 228 measures
   Technique: arpeggios, fast scale runs, trills,
    octaves (broken and double), repeated notes

VARIATIONS, D Major,   <u>Advancing Intermediate</u>
  Hob.XVII:7 (before 1766) (Five Variations)

GERLACH, Sonja: Haydn Klavierstücke--Urtext
  (G. Henle Verlag).

  The tedious theme of these <u>Variations</u> makes the
whole set uninteresting. However, the piece could be
used to introduce the variation form. The only difficulties are the scalar figures in variation 2 and broken
chords in variation 5.

   Tempo: Andante
   Length: 90 measures
   Technique: scales, arpeggios, syncopation,
    broken chords

ADAGIO, F Major, Hob.XVII:9 (1786)   <u>Intermediate</u>

ALFRED (Publisher): Haydn--15 of his Most Popular...
BANOWETZ, Joseph: Pianist's Book of Classic Treasures
    (Kjos).
GERLACH, Sonja: Haydn Klavierstücke--Urtext
    (G. Henle Verlag).
WEITZMAN, Fritz: Easiest Piano Pieces
    (Peters No. 5004).

The true galant style of this piece is characterized
by simplicity and elegance. The rhythm requires careful
attention, but otherwise this <u>Adagio</u> is accessible and
enjoyable.   The pianist should be aware of melodic
voicing, articulation, and dynamics.
        Length: 30 measures
        Technique: slow scales and arpeggios, dotted
            rhythms

II. SONATAS

The keyboard sonatas of Haydn occupy a prominent position in the catalogue of the composer's works. Written over a period extending from the years of earliest activity until 1795, the sonatas provide a fascinating record of the composer's style and artistic personality. The diversity found among these works is staggering, and while less influential than the symphonies and string quartets, the sonatas are a rich and compelling testament to Haydn's inventive faculties. The intimate medium of the solo sonata allowed Haydn freedom to use the genre as a vehicle for continuous formal experimentation, and they are among their creator's most personal utterances. However, a full emotional gamut is found in these works, and profound movements of consummate craftsmanship coexist with light, galant pieces of a purely superficial nature. Seldom has a single aspect of a composer's output revealed so wide a spectrum of quality, form, and content. The sonatas are saturated in the varied manifestations of the composer's complex artistic personality, and form a remarkably complete and comprehensive chronicle of Haydn's multi-faceted genius.

The earliest multi-movement keyboard compositions of Haydn, (originally entitled "divertimenti" or "partitas," as Haydn did not use the term "sonata" until 1773), are greatly indebted to the many divertimenti of Georg Christoph Wagenseil (1715-1777). Wagenseil, the leading Viennese composer of Haydn's youth, was a capable and popular creator of pieces in an elegant and genial galant style. The divertimenti of Wagenseil are notable for crisp homophonic textures, straightforward harmonies and harmonic rhythms, simple multi-movement structures based on dance forms, and a delightfully titillating rococo sensibility marked by a casual lyric grace. The movements in binary form exhibit many of the traits of the sonata/allegro genre, yet lack any strong sense of dialectic based on contrasting musical ideas. Development is often rudimentary and, like the earlier suite, these unassuming compositions display an almost total unity of key. Generally in three movements, these divertimenti often conclude with a minuet.

Haydn's divertimenti of the period prior to the mid-1760's possess all of these attributes and differ from Wagenseil's primarily in a less pronounced tendency to indulge in unyieldingly regular phrase structure and predictable harmonic procedures. Haydn displays a greater and more engaging melodic and formal inventiveness. Using the partita framework inherited from Wagenseil and his contemporaries, Haydn was able to fashion vivacious and spirited works which fully express the more jovial aspects of the composer's character. Haydn's earliest keyboard sonatas lack consistent inspiration and technical command, yet they contain all the salient features of the Viennese galant style, and accurately and fetchingly reveal the composer's playful and ingratiating spirit.

Haydn's artistic development was a lengthy and gradual process of evolution, and a clear division of his work into rigidly self-contained stylistic periods is difficult, if not futile. However, by 1767 the influence of C.P.E. Bach (1714-1788) and the North German school of sonata composers becomes more immediately recognizable. A fuller and more highly developed use of the sonata/allegro principle is typical of this period. The dialogue of contrasting themes, as the vivifying element of this form is apparent, and the development section is more extensive and elaborate. Traces of both the "empfindsamer Stil" and the volatile proto-romantic "Sturm und Drang" movements begin to appear in Haydn's work. The empfindsamer (sensitive) influence is found in the delicate, occasionally overwrought and precious ornamentation of the slow movements, the widely expanded harmonic vocabulary, and in the air of gentle tenderness and pathos. The lyrical impulse, generally lacking in Haydn's earlier works, is more effectively realized in the compositions of this period. The late 1760's and early 1770's witnessed many important changes in Haydn's use of the sonata form. The works of these years make extensive use of large scale sonata/allegro designs, tonal variety among movements, more complex harmonic procedures, and an expanded scope and emotional depth.

By 1773 Haydn had fully assimilated both the Italianate galanterie of Wagenseil and the Germanic breadth and structural expressivity of C.P.E Bach, to achieve a fully personal synthesis. During this period of absolute formal and expressive mastery Haydn's position as the preeminent composer of his generation was firmly established. Though Haydn composed fewer solo sonatas during this time, those that date from these years of complete maturity reveal a thorough craftsmanship with a subtle, if lively, inspiration. These important works are the foundation without which many of the sonatas of Haydn's great successors would be inconceivable.

Haydn's art was continually undergoing creative transformation, and the great variety found in the sonatas is evidence of this process. Although Haydn is often credited with the final stabilization of the sonata form, the diversity found within the composer's own oeuvre reveals a fertile imagination not content with formulaic repetition. Typically, many of Haydn's first movements deviate from the standard sonata/allegro pattern.

Among the movements in sonata/allegro form, there are innumerable irregularities that add piquant charm and interest. Haydn is noted for "monothematic" sonata/allegros in which the structure corresponds to the standard format, yet the contrast between the thematic material of each key group is not clearly differentiated. The term "monothematic" is perhaps inaccurate as these movements usually exhibit a super-abundance of musical materials, and are "monothematic" only in the sense that the traditional "masculine/feminine" thematic dicotomy is blurred and indistinct. Haydn often inserts bridge passages of considerable complexity and length as well as using substantial closing sections and codas. New material is introduced to create dramatic effects and the composer constantly abbreviates, rearranges, and develops the recapitulation. Haydn uses the traditional sonata/allegro as a foil against which to display a daring and brilliant musical rhetoric, at its best characterized by overwhelming variety and dazzling inventiveness.

Extended variation forms, on both single and double themes, are occasionally used to open a sonata. There are a number of two-movement works in which an initial set of variations is followed by a spirited finale. Haydn established the rondo as the basic structural pattern for the closing movement of a sonata, yet this model is not invariably followed. Several sonatas conclude with theme and variations or movements in sonata/allegro form. The minuet was a form cultivated with particular success by Haydn, and among the dances in this style found in the sonatas, several are used as closing movements. Even among the rondos there is a marked preference for themes that are rhythmically and stylistically related to the minuet.

The finest of Haydn's keyboard sonatas reveal many of the composer's unique and distinctive mannerisms. The extreme rhythmic verve and complexity which sets Haydn apart from his contemporaries is a vital element of these works. Phrase structure is rich and imaginatively varied. Elaborately figured slow movements are featured, and though they may occasionally exude an aura of florid monotony, the adagios of Haydn's later sonatas have the poise and pathos characteristic of his mature style. The boisterous vivacity for which Haydn is so beloved is often found in the sonatas, as is a hearty elegance, and rarest of all, a profound joy.

SONATA, D Major, Hob.XIV:5   <u>Advancing Intermediate</u>
(c.1765/66)

Moderato

The Landon edition publishes the surviving fragment of this sonata/allegro, and includes a reconstruction of the movement by the editor and Karl Heinz Fussl. The autograph fragment containing much of the recapitulation has been provided with an effective exposition based on the entry for this work in Haydn's holograph thematic catalogue. The development section is attractive and stylistically accurate. A stirring martial character and bright good spirit characterize this work. The technical demands are slight and the keyboard is used quite idiomatically.

> Tempo: Moderato
> Length: 65 measures
> Technique: double 3rds and 6ths, simple
>   syncopation, scales, scalar passages,
>   octaves, ornaments

Menuet and Trio

A turbulent and dramatic Trio creates a poignant contrast to the simple lyricism of this gracefully figured Menuet. There are few rhythmic problems and the work is well within the range of the less mature pianist.

> Length: 88 measures
> Technique: octaves, double 3rds, simple
>   syncopation, easy figuration

SONATA, C Major, Hob.XVI/1   Advancing Intermediate
    (before 1766)

Allegro

A lively and driving movement, this <u>Allegro</u> provides many opportunities for creative dynamic nuance and contrast.   Constant motivic repetition requires careful melodic shaping. The Alberti bass is relentless and should be subdued.

> Length: 50 measures
> Technique: Alberti bass, ornaments,
>   figuration

Adagio

The beautiful melody and elegant character of this <u>Adagio</u> can be brought out by sensitive phrase shaping. The piece is accessible and provides a good study in melodic phrasing.

> Length: 17 measures
> Technique: scalar passages, repeated notes,
>   constant R.H. 16th note triplet figuration

Menuet and Trio

The success of this sonata can be attributed to the fact that each movement has a completely different character, yet they form a cohesive whole.   This particular Menuet is of a very light nature, while the Trio is in a darker vein. Technical hurdles are avoided and it is quite enjoyable to play.

> Length: 43 measures
> Technique: R.H. continuous offbeat to L.H.
>   melody

SONATA, G Major, Hob. XVI/G1   Intermediate
   (before 1766)

Allegro

No serious rhythmic or technical problems are encountered in this unsophisticated and approachable movement. There are many easy five finger patterns, but sloppy articulations should be avoided. Alberti bass figures must be subdued.

> Length: 80 measures
> Technique: broken intervals, double notes,
>   scalar passages, ornaments, 16th note
>   triplets, 32nd notes

Menuet and Trio

A simple charm characterizes this unpretentious movement.

> Length: 46 measures
> Technique: broken octaves, double notes,
>   scales, ornaments

Finale

An attractive foil to the previous movement, the Finale has no rhythmic problems and contains contrasting styles and characters which maintain interest. It is fast and joyful with a middle section in the parallel minor. This piece also serves as the opening movement of the Sonata in G Major, Hob. XVI/11.

> Tempo: Presto
> Length: 48 measures
> Technique: octaves, broken intervals,
>   ornaments

SONATA, Bb Major, Hob.XVI:2   <u>Early Advanced</u>
  (before 1766)

Moderato

Many two-note phrases and a variety of creative textures are found in this movement. It is a delightful piece to play and can help the pianist develop sensitivity to phrase structure and voicing.

> Length: 148 measures
> Technique: double notes, scalar figures,
>   sustained and moving notes,
>   and .

Largo (G Minor)

The Largo is in a dramatic aria style, with a lyrical melody containing several cadenza-like figures. The complex rhythms must be supported by a steady pulse.

> Length: 54 measures
>
> Technique: scalar figures, complex rhythms, sustained and moving notes, ornaments, trills

Menuet and Trio

A lively spirit is found in this delightful Menuet. Typical of Haydn, the somber Trio in Bb minor evokes a contrasting mood.

> Length: 56 measures
>
> Technique: coordinating contrasting rhythms

SONATA, D Minor, Hob.XVI:2a (c.1765-66)

Note: Sonatas Hob.XVI:2a-2h survive only in the form of brief fragments from Haydn's holograph "Entwurf-Katalogue."

SONATA, A Major, Hob.XVI:2b (c.1765-66)

SONATA, B Major, Hob.XVI:2c (c.1765-66)

SONATA, Bb Major, Hob.XVI:2d (c.1765-66)

SONATA, E Minor, Hob.XVI:2e (c.1765-66)

SONATA, C Major, Hob.XVI:2g (c.1765-66)

SONATA, A Major, Hob.XVI:2h (c.1765-66)

SONATA, C Major, Hob.XVI/3   <u>Advancing Intermediate</u>
(before 1766)

Allegretto

A dull <u>Allegretto</u>, this work suffers from a bland melody and incessant legato broken chord triplets which soon become monotonous.   Subtle nuances, whether dynamic or articulative, will make the piece more interesting.

       Length: 84 measures
       Technique: ornaments, broken triads,
         4 against 3

Andante (G Major)

Playful invention is displayed in this stately <u>Andante</u>.   To prevent tedium, the pianist should shape each melody, bring out the contrapuntal lines, and maintain rhythmic accuracy.

       Length: 79 measures
       Technique: slow scales, complex rhythms,
         ornaments

Menuet and Trio

A representative Haydn minuet, this is the strongest movement in the sonata. The Trio emphasizes mood changes and lovely phrase shapes.
> Length: 50 measures
> Technique: ornaments

SONATA, D Major, Hob.XVI/4   Early Intermediate
(before 1766)

Moderato

The elegant character of this cohesive and pianistic movement demands a light touch. It is virtuosic, with broken interval figurations, sixteenth note triplet scalar figures, and arpeggios. Melodic lines in the figurations should be stressed, and care should be taken to maintain a consistent tempo.
> Length: 57 measures
> Technique: brokan intervals, 16th-note triplet
>   scalar figures, arpeggios, ornaments

Menuet and Trio

As with many of Haydn's dance movements, the minuet and trio form a distinct antithesis. This particular Menuet is stately and straightforward, while the Trio is more subdued. There are no technical problems, though a few rhythmic difficulties occur due to dotted notes and triplets.

> Length: 44 measures
> Technique: triplets, sudden register shifts,
>   broken 3rds, trills

SONATA, A Major, Hob. XVI/5   Early Advanced
  (before 1763)

Allegro

Pure tactile enjoyment will ensue after the difficult figurations and line shapings are mastered. This brilliant and energetic Allegro demands dexterity. Relaxation and a steady tempo will facilitate performance.

> Length: 141 measures
> Technique: scales, broken intervals, double
>   notes, Alberti bass, octaves, arpeggios

Menuet and Trio

This simple respite from the two difficult outer movements provides an opportunity to shape lines and phrases. The darker nature of the Trio necessitates a complete dynamic change.

> Length: 40 measures
> Technique: double notes, ornaments, scales

Presto

Deceptive difficulty is encountered in this delicate sounding Presto. Many ornaments and wide leaps may cause problems. The mode changes project diverse characters. Several passages would be enhanced by an echo effect. Most authorities question the authenticity of this delightful sonata.

> Length: 129 measures
> Technique: repeated notes, arpeggios, double
>   notes, scales, ornaments, octaves, leaps,
>   broken octaves

SONATA, G Major, Hob.XVI/6   Early Advanced
   (before 1766)

Allegro

The major obstacle in this Allegro is the tremendous rhythmic diversity. The ever-shifting beat division makes it difficult to achieve a smooth flow. The rhythms are combined with troublesome technical problems such as fast scales and trills. Creative dynamics and articulations will provide interest.

> Length: 47 measures
> Technique: fast scales, trills, leaps, repeated
>   double notes, 2 against 3, octaves,
>   arpeggiated grace notes

Menuet and Trio

Rhythmically precise dotted rhythms will enhance the courtly character of this Menuet. The Trio alternates ornamented duplets with triplets and is an excellent opportunity for dynamic echoes and melodic shaping.

>   Length: 58 measures
>   Technique: ornaments, alternating duplets and
>   triplets, octaves, sustained and moving
>   notes

Adagio (G Minor)

Although harmonically drab in spots, the florid aria-like melodies make this a lovely and compelling Adagio. Careful shaping will reveal an expressive lyricism. The Landon edition gives some excellent suggestions for fermata ornamentation.

>   Length: 25 measures
>   Technique: ornaments, L.H. melody in 3rds,
>   scalar figures, extended trill, repeated
>   intervals

Finale

The brilliant final movement is quite difficult, though once mastered it is fun to play. It could be used as an etude for several technical skills such as arpeggios and scales.

Tempo: Allegro Molto
Length: 90 measures
Technique: arpeggios, scales, ornaments,
    octaves, broken octaves

SONATA, C Major, Hob.XVI/7   Advancing Intermediate
    (before 1766)

Allegro Moderato

Rather difficult, this spirited piece is very satisfying to play. The brisk martial character lends itself to a creative use of dynamics and articulations. Technical difficulties such as rapid scales and weak finger trills will tax the less experienced pianist, as will the interchange of quarter, eighth, and 32nd notes.

Length: 23 measures
Technique: trills, repeated notes, scales

Menuet and Trio

Scalar figures requiring careful fingering are the major technical challenge in this tuneful and interesting Menuet. The left hand has the melody in the Trio, where clarity of voicing is crucial.

Length: 37 measures
Technique: scales, voicing

Finale

The Finale is the most difficult and harmonically interesting movement of the sonata. There are several instances of two against three, and fast, lengthy broken octaves. Attention to detail will enhance the lively character of this piece.

Tempo: Allegro
Length: 55 measures
Technique: broken octaves, 2 against 3,
    broken intervals, trills, scalar passages

SONATA, G Major, Hob.XVI/8   <u>Intermediate</u>
    (before 1766)

Allegro

This lively movement has an agreeable two-voice texture. Deceptively tricky, it presents rhythmic problems such as triplets surrounded by duplets and off-beat patterns.

Length: 44 measures
Technique: repeated notes, ornaments,
    contrapuntal lines, broken intervals,
    rhythmic variety, sustained and moving
    notes, 16th note triplets

Menuet

As in the first movement, rhythmic complexity is the main obstacle. In the first four measures half notes, quarter notes, eighth notes, eighth note triplets, and sixteenth notes are encountered.

Length: 16 measures
Technique: scales, broken triads, ornaments

Andante

Melodic and well balanced, this warm and compact Andante would be an appropriate introduction to Haydn's slow movements.

Length: 9 measures
Technique: contrapuntal lines, scales,
ornaments

Allegro

There are no particular rhythmic problems in this fast and jocund movement. The broken interval accompaniment should be subdued. This <u>Allegro</u> is a good study in finger independence and facility.

    Length: 24 measures

    Technique: broken interval figuration, octaves, sustained and moving notes

SONATA, F Major, Hob.XVI/9   <u>Advancing Intermediate</u>
  (before 1766)

Allegro

Resembling Scarlatti, this sprightly movement has attractive, virtuosic figuration and ornamentation. The tricky rhythm demands careful attention. There are many possibilities for dynamic effects, including echoes.

    Length: 42 measures

    Technique: octaves, ornaments

Menuet and Trio

The light effect of this <u>Menuet</u> must be maintained, in spite of the many octaves. Interlaced duple and triple figures may be a rhythmic problem. This movement can be very expressive if dynamics are used to achieve transformations of mood and color. Each contrapuntal line should be heard clearly and independently.

    Length: 44 measures

    Technique: ornaments, octaves

Scherzo

An effective contrast to the Menuet and Trio, this familiar movement is fast and animated but not difficult. The left hand sixteenth notes should be subdued, emphasizing the ascending melodic figures. This familiar piece is extremely pianistic and enjoyable to play.

Tempo: Allegro
Length: 24 measures
Technique: broken intervals, scalar passages

SONATA, C Major, Hob.XVI/10   Advancing Intermediate
(before 1766)

Moderato

Diversity is created through the use of varied touches and dynamics in this playful movement in sonata form.   Rhythmic problems include triplets, thirty-second notes, and the many taxing ornaments. A relaxed tempo is essential.

Length: 59 measures
Technique: ornaments, trills, 32nd notes,
   turns

Menuet and Trio

A playful character similar to the first movement marks this colorfully ornamented Menuet. In comparison, the Trio is darkly expressive. There are no major difficulties in this fine work which is useful for developing dynamic nuance and sensitivity

      Length: 44 measures

      Technique: ornaments, sustained and moving
         notes

Finale

Brilliant and full of spirit, this movement is gratifying to play. Close attention to fingering and dynamics is important in passages containing rapid figuration. The many countermelodies should be stressed.

      Tempo: Presto

      Length: 94 measures

      Technique: broken intervals, broken triads,
         scales, octaves

SONATA, G Major, Hob.XVI/11 <u>Advancing Intermediate</u>

Presto

The last movement of the earlier <u>Sonata in G</u>, Hob. XVI/G1 is an exact duplicate of this <u>Presto</u>. It is fast and joyful and is an excellent etude in finger facility. Lightly played octaves will maintain the fleeting character of the piece. The beautiful second section can be highlighted by discerning dynamic changes.

> Length: 48 measures
> Technique: octaves, broken intervals,
>   ornaments

Andante (G Minor)

Lovely melodies and unusual harmonies mark this beautiful <u>Andante</u> in sonata form. Close attention to expressive nuance will reveal the graceful phrase structure.

> Length: 63 measures
> Technique: octaves, ornaments, broken 3rds

Menuet and Trio

Both <u>Minuet and Trio</u> have a quaint bucolic quality. To convey the lively rustic character, the pulse should be felt as one beat per measure. Occasional eighth note arpeggios are the only technical demand. The performer should articulate crisply and smoothly. This is an excellent and accessible sonata, providing ample opportunity for virtuosic, yet sensitive, playing.

> Tempo: Allegretto
> Length: 55 measures
> Technique: arpeggios, simple Alberti bass

SONATA, A Major, Hob.XVI/12   Advancing Intermediate
(before 1766)

Andante

This diverting movement is reminiscent of early Mozart. The symmetrical theme is supported by accompanimental triplets. Elegance and grace are expressed in the long trills and ornaments. The performer should be sensitive to the dynamic shape of the ascending and descending lines.

> Length: 55 measures
> Technique: arpeggios, scales, ornaments,
>   extended trill, sustained and moving notes

Menuet and Trio

In most of Haydn's minuet and trio movements, the trio is a foil to the minuet. In this instance, the contrast is stunning. The Menuet is simple, flowing, and unassuming, while the Trio (in the parallel minor) is poignant and dramatic. This movement is a good study in musicality, and an excellent selection for an advancing elementary or early intermediate adult who has limited technical ability.

> Length: 54 measures
> Technique: offbeat R.H. against steady L.H.
>   quarter notes, sustained and moving notes

Finale

The clear and propulsive Finale epitomizes the Haydn style. Replete with interesting mode changes and clever configurations, it is an appropriate ending to the sonata as it blithely mitigates the dramatic tension of the Menuet.

> Tempo: Allegro molto
> Length: 69 measures
> Technique: Alberti bass, scales, arpeggios,
>   mordents

SONATA, E Major, Hob.XVI/13 Advancing Intermediate
   (before 1766)

Moderato

Rhythmic precision is essential in this movement. The unassuming moderato demands dynamic nuance and creative articulation. The technical problems include many ornaments which must fit into a small division of the beat.

> Length: 84 measures
> Technique: scales, ornaments, repeated notes,
>   sustained and moving notes

Menuet and Trio

A particularly delightful <u>Trio</u> crowns this attractive
<u>Menuet.</u>   It is also a good trill etude without other
technical difficulties.

> Length: 52 measures
> Technique: scales, octaves, trills, sustained
>   and moving notes, appoggiaturas

Finale

Haydn's jovial good nature is evident in this brilliant
movement.   The many figurations are not difficult.
Finger independence and evenness are required in this
accessible and spirited presto.

> Tempo: Presto
> Length: 107 measures
> Technique: various figurations, scales, broken
>   triads, double 3rds, steady tempo

SONATA, D Major, Hob.XVI/14   <u>Early Advanced</u>
   (before 1766)

Allegro Moderato

Rhythmically vital, this charming movement is very engaging. It contains constantly shifting rhythms, a variety of dotted figures, and two against three. The passage work is fluent and not difficult.
   Length: 110 measures
   Technique: scales, fast runs, various
        figurations, complex rhythms, repeated 3rds,
        sustained and moving notes

Menuet and Trio

The <u>Menuet</u> is in a galant light-hearted style, while the <u>Trio</u> is more serious. The entire movement is harmonically inventive and quite interesting. Sustained and moving notes are the only major technical difficulty.
   Length: 55 measures
   Technique: scales, arpeggios, sustained and
        moving notes, extended trills, double 3rds

Finale

The dramatic <u>Finale</u> is the strongest movement of the sonata. It is very pianistic, and the numerous figurations require finger facility. There are many opportunites for dynamic contrast.

> Tempo: Allegro
> Length: 108 measures
> Technique: arpeggios, scales, Alberti bass, ornaments, sustained and moving notes, double 3rds, octaves

SONATA, Eb Major, Hob.XVI:16   <u>Intermediate</u>
   (before 1766)

Andante

An unusual use of the sonata/allegro principle characterizes this problematic movement. A standard distribution of key is apparent in the exposition, yet the first theme group (tonic) is at an "andante" tempo while the second (dominant) is marked "presto." The short development section is followed by an abbreviated recapitulation. Though the musical material lacks distinction, the tempo changes and two cadenzas create an interesting improvisatory effect.

> Length: 75 measures
> Technique: trills, ornaments, scales, double 3rds, repeated note figuration, octaves

Menuet and Trio

Rhythmic diversity is the most notable aspect of this vital dance. The basic pulse is divided into ♩.♪ , ♩♪♪ , and ♪♪.figures. The <u>Trio</u>, in the relative minor, is attractive and exploits hand crossing.

> Length: 48 measures
> Technique: hand-crossing, scalar passages,
>   octaves, repeated double 3rds, legato L.H.
>   and R.H. offbeat interval accompaniment.

Presto

Sparkling and brisk, this rudimentary sonata/allegro contains some simple and attractive scalar and broken chord figuration. The piece is not technically demanding and is musically straightforward. Though intriguing, this curious sonata is not representative of Haydn, and its authenticity is generally questioned.

> Length: 51 measures
> Technique: scalar passages, broken chord
>   figuration, broken octaves, trills, double
>   3rds

SONATA, Bb Major, Hob.XVI/18   Advanced
(ca. 1766/1767)

Allegro Moderato

In traditional sonata/allegro form, this movement is harmonically inventive. Two major performance problems are found: many ornaments are contained within a small area of the beat, and the rhythm is constantly shifting between thirty-second and sixteenth notes. Effective dynamics and a steady tempo will enhance this captivating piece.

> Length: 117 measures
> Technique: fast scalar and passage work,
>   sustained and moving notes, ornaments

Moderato

Musical style warrants much attention in this introspective movement. Creative shaping of the phrases will emphasize the subdued minuet-like character of this beautiful piece.

> Length: 110 measures
> Technique: double 3rds, broken 3rds, scales,
>   ornaments, sustained and moving notes,
>   contrapuntal textures, voicing

SONATA, D Major, Hob.XVI:19 (1767)   Early Advanced

Moderato

Haydn cleverly develops several themes and unifies them in an ingenuous and captivating manner. An important distinction must be made between ♩♩♩ and ♪♪♩. The pianist should bring out the melody and activate the inherent rhythmic vitality.

> Length: 102 measures
> Technique: rhythmic variety, finger facility,
>   scales, broken intervals, repeated notes

Andante (A Major)

Imaginative articulations are required in this intricate and unique movement. The left hand melody must be carefully marked. The many register changes add to the character of the piece. The Landon edition includes an effective fermata embellishment.

> Length: 115 measures
> Technique: double notes, scales, ornaments,
>   large leaps

Finale

The Finale is dramatic, driving, harmonically inventive, texturally varied, and full of riotous good humor. The many bass figures are useful for developing left hand finger facility. This is an extremely suc-cessful sonata with every movement of equal strength.

> Tempo: Allegro Assai
> Length: 125 measures
> Technique: various 16th note figurations,
>   broken octaves, ornaments, octaves, scalar
>   passages, Alberti bass

SONATA, C Minor, Hob.XVI:20 (1771)   Advanced

Moderato

Intense and emotional, this innovative work displays exciting harmonies and ever-changing textures. A creative use of dynamics and articulations is essential in this dramatic and pathos-filled movement. The mature pianist will find this great work an interpretative challenge.

> Length: 100 measures
> Technique: double notes (octaves, 3rds),
>   scales, arpeggios, broken triads, broken
>   octaves, ornaments

Andante con moto (Ab Major)

Although still dramatic, the lighter Andante is a respite from the intensity of the previous movement. The ornaments are not as difficult as those often found in Haydn's works. The occasional syncopation adds piquant rhythmic verve.

> Length: 67 measures
> Technique: ornaments, scales, double 3rds,
>   sustained and moving notes, syncopation,
>   voicing

Finale

Dark but spirited, this movement is technically less demanding than the other two. The many sixteenth note figurations are not difficult. This fine sonata is among Haydn's most profoundly moving compositions.

> Tempo: Allegro
> Length: 152 measures
> Technique: 16th-note figurations, hand-
>   crossing, sustained and moving notes,
>   broken octaves, double 3rds

SONATA, C Major, Hob.XVI:21 (1773)   Early Advanced

Allegro

This prosaic Allegro is pervaded by continuous dotted rhythms. Occasional triplets partially mitigate the monotony. These two rhythmic figures should be carefully differentiated.

> Length: 149 measures
> Technique: scales, arpeggios, broken octaves,
>   ornaments, sustained and moving notes

Adagio (F Major)

On initial inspection this <u>Adagio</u> may appear overly diffuse, yet further examination reveals ample musical content. Many cadenza-like scalar figures contribute to the elegance of this arioso.

> Length: 64 measures
> Technique: scales (cadenza-like figures),
>   octaves, double 3rds, repeated notes

Finale

The jovial <u>Finale</u> is full of pep and drive. The pianist must ensure evenness of the many figurations and highlight each contrapuntal line. Few rhythmic or technical problems occur in this brilliant and effective movement.

> Tempo: Presto
> Length: 124 measures
> Technique: arpeggios, broken intervals,
>   ornaments

SONATA, E Major, Hob.XVI:22 (1773)   <u>Advanced</u>

Allegro Moderato

Reminiscent of early Beethoven, this fine movement contains dramatic pauses and shifting accents. Many of the technical aspects, such as ornaments, are difficult and would be good practice for finger facility. The piece requires careful shaping of phrases and contrapuntal lines.

Length: 75 measures
Technique: ornaments, repeated notes,
    arpeggios, broken triads

Andante (E Minor)

Thoughtful attention to detail will enhance this lyrical <u>Andante.</u> An effective slow movement, it is charming and emotionally moving.

Length: 69 measures
Technique: sustained and moving notes,
    broken octaves

Finale

The structurally interesting <u>Finale</u> combines elements of both the variation and rondo forms. The themes are rather innocuous, but a lively performance will provide a charming conclusion to this elegant sonata.

Tempo: Tempo di Menuet
Length: 108 measures
Technique: scalar passages, arpeggios,
    ornaments, double notes, sustained and
    moving notes

SONATA, F Major, Hob.XVI:23 (1773)   <u>Early Advanced</u>

Moderato

Buoyant and cohesive, this exciting movement employs unique harmonies. Many different figurations provide an excellent study in finger facility.

      Length: 127 measures

      Technique: scales, trills, arpeggios, octaves, various 32nd-note figurations, careful articulation

Adagio (F Minor)

Careful phrasing and creative dynamics will enhance the intense beauty of this poignant and introspective <u>Adagio</u>.

      Length: 39 measures

      Technique: ornaments, arpeggios

Finale

This subtle yet lively movement is the perfect conclusion to the sonata. The contrapuntal passages demand careful attention, and the entire work requires some technical skill.

Tempo: Presto
Length: 147 measures
Technique: double notes, arpeggios, scales,
   various figurations, articulations

SONATA, D Major, Hob.XVI:24 (1773)   <u>Early Advanced</u>

Allegro

A very light and spirited character marks this <u>Allegro</u>. The occasional chromaticism and creative harmonies provide interest. The many figurations, including scales and arpeggios, call for rapid finger facility.

Length: 155 measures
Technique: arpeggios, scales, double notes,
   ornaments, broken intervals, various
   figurations

Adagio (D Minor)

As with many of Haydn's slow movements, this florid <u>Adagio</u> is reminiscent of an operatic aria. There are no rhythmic problems, though a steady sense of pulse is essential.

Length: 37 measures
Technique: scales and fast runs, left hand
   double notes

Finale

The Finale reveals Haydn at his most playful. Unusual syncopations displace the beat and create rhythmic vitality. The entire sonata is typical of the composer and well-suited to performance.

     Tempo: Presto

     Length: 111 measures

     Technique: double notes, scales, broken triads
        divided between the hands, syncopation,

SONATA, Eb Major, Hob.XVI:25 (1773)   Advanced

Moderato

Although the themes are rather mundane, the movement is salvaged by clever and exciting development through extensive figuration. A thoughtful use of dynamics will create a more cohesive effect.

     Length: 71 measures

     Technique: broken intervals, scales, double
        notes, ornaments, trill figures, complex
        rhythms

Tempo di Menuet

This movement is a canon of considerable charm and interest. Motivic use of the rhythmic figures should be emphasized. The entire sonata is unpretentious and witty.

Length: 44 measures
Technique: scales, ornaments

SONATA, A Major, Hob.XVI:26 (1773)   Advanced

Allegro Moderato

A powerful movement, this <u>Allegro</u> contains some of Haydn's finest writing for the piano. The prevalent dotted rhythms are neither dull nor static and are united with beautiful harmonies. Smooth transitions are attained by employing sustained and moving notes within the circle of fifths. The exciting development contains the tremendous climax--a dramatic and expansive spinning out of the motives.

Length: 82 measures
Technique: arpeggios, scales, ornaments,
      sustained and moving notes, broken octaves

Menuet al Rovescio and Trio

The <u>Menuet</u> provides a charming and simple contrast to the first movement. "Al Rovescio" means "reversed" --both halves of the <u>Menuet</u> and the <u>Trio</u> are mirrors of each other. It is fascinating to examine how Haydn accomplished this with a logical and beautiful result. The double notes are relatively simple.

> Length: 44 measures
> Technique: simple double notes

Finale

The short and attractive <u>Finale</u> is a diverting study on the A Major scale. It is lively and effortless and is the perfect conclusion to a delightful sonata.

> Tempo: Presto
> Length: 26 measures
> Technique: scales

SONATA, G Major, Hob.XVI:27   <u>Advancing Intermediate</u>
  (1776)

Allegro Con Brio

The perennial popularity of this movement is due to its considerable musical effectiveness. It is pianistic, with scale runs, Alberti bass, and broken octaves. As it is quite a spirited piece, the "con brio" should be taken literally. The development section is strong and dramatic, creating effective contrasts.

> Length: 143 measures
> Technique: scalar runs, Alberti bass, broken
>   octaves, broken 3rds, ornaments

Menuet and Trio

Broken chords and noteworthy fermatas provide interest in this unusual <u>Menuet</u>. Creative articulation will enliven the many repeated phrases. The <u>Trio</u> is expressive and includes many embellishments.

> Length: 66 measures
> Technique: broken triads, double notes,
>   ornaments

Finale

An ideal ending for the sonata, this lively <u>Finale</u> in a modified variation form has an abundance of elaborate figuration. The theme is energetic with a variety of articulations. The musical content is vivacious with chromatic interest. The entire work is a good introduction to Haydn's keyboard sonatas.

> Tempo: Presto
> Length: 152 measures
> Technique: broken intervals, arpeggios, scales

SONATA, Eb Major, Hob.XVI:28 (1776)   Early Advanced

Allegro Moderato

This engaging Allegro is simple and unpretentious. While not difficult, it is challenging enough to hold the pianist's interest. Care must be given to dynamics for a vital performance.

> Length: 155 measures
> Technique: ornaments, hand-crossing, scales,
>   double notes, broken 3rds

Menuet and Trio

The Menuet is an elegantly ornamented piece with many triplets. The Trio, in the parallel minor, is of a darker character with an insistent eighth note motive. The contrast between the two sections should be heightened.

> Length: 48 measures
> Technique: scales, ornaments

Finale

The rondo-like Finale entertains a clever theme characterized by charming and pianistic variations. Finger facility and hand independence are essential in this amusing work.

> Tempo: Presto
> Length: 172 measures
> Technique: scales, double notes, arpeggios,
> various 16th note figurations

SONATA, F Major, Hob.XVI:29 (1774)   <u>Early Advanced</u>

Moderato

Broad in scope and content, this movement contains diverse textures. The constantly changing character requires a sensitive pianist who can accommodate the rapid shifts of mood.

> Length: 90 measures
> Technique: arpeggios, scales, ornaments, 32nd
> and 64th notes

Adagio (Bb Major)

Mature phrasing and the imaginative use of dynamics will help avoid monotony in this protracted movement. The ornate lyricism is suggestive of Mozart.

> Length: 36 measures
> Technique: Alberti bass, scales, repeated
> notes, double notes, ornaments

Tempo di Menuet

This curious ending to the sonata is not particularly boisterous or conclusive. While technically approachable, several cross-rhythms and beat displacements make this fascinating movement deceptively complex.

Length: 99 measures
Technique: scales, arpeggios, double notes,
ornaments, cross-rhythms

SONATA, A Major, Hob.XVI:30 (1776)   Early Advanced

Allegro

A touch of the galant is found in this playful movement, characterized by dotted rhythms and brilliant figurations. The unusual Adagio coda functions as a slow movement, providing a link to the Tempo di Minuet.

Length: 183 measures
Technique: broken octaves, scales, arpeggios,
double notes

Tempo di Menuet (with 6 variations)

There are few memorable musical features in this unassuming set of variations. However, the theme is pleasant and the variations have a rococo charm. Variation 5 is the most effective.

> Length: 128 measures
> Technique: scales, arpeggios, double 3rds,
>   sustained and moving notes

SONATA, E Major, Hob.XVI:31 (1776)   <u>Early Advanced</u>

Moderato

This sensitive work has a graceful, contrapuntal opening. Care should be taken to expose the left hand melodies and subdue the right hand accompaniments. The interesting modulations, scalar passages, and lovely melodies make this movement a delightful musical experience.

> Length: 65 measures
> Technique: arpeggios, trills, ornaments,
>   melody in double notes, various 16th
>   note triplet figurations, voicing,
>   scalar passages

Allegretto (E Minor)

Beautiful and harmonically intriguing, this movement demands a relaxed tempo. The entire work is extremely contrapuntal, and Haydn uses a variety of compositional devices such as invertible counterpoint and numerous suspensions. This fine movement tests the pianist's sensitivity to articulation and voicing.

Length: 47 measures
Technique: sustained and moving notes,
    double 3rds, articulations, voicing

Finale

The light character of this movement provides a brilliant ending to the sonata. The technical difficulties are compounded by numerous fast ornaments and awkward figurations.

Tempo: Presto
Length: 101 measures
Technique: scales, arpeggios, trills, octaves,
    finger facility, double 3rds, broken octaves

SONATA, B Minor, Hob.XVI:32 (1776)   Advanced

Allegro Moderato

Drama and intriguing harmonies combine to make this work a highpoint of Haydn's creative output. The technical elements are rather difficult, but once learned, the piece is a pleasure to play.

Length: 70 measures
Technique: broken intervals, ornaments,
    scales, sustained and moving notes,
    substitution fingering

Menuet (B Major)

The extended <u>Menuet</u> is stately and beautiful. The middle section contains some of the "Sturm und Drang" characteristics found in the first movement. Because of the tempo, there are no major technical difficulties, although fingerings should be carefully planned.

> Tempo: Tempo di Menuet
> Length: 62 measures
> Technique: scales, ornaments, broken
>   intervals, trills

Finale

The excellent and well-crafted <u>Finale</u> is full of intense and unique ideas, and includes such compositional devices as invertible counterpoint and canon. It is concise, yet powerful, concluding a passionate sonata marked by drama and intensity.

> Tempo: Presto
> Length: 193 measures
> Technique: double notes, scalar figures,
>   scales, octaves

SONATA, D Major, Hob.XVI:33   <u>Early Advanced</u>
(ca. 1771/1773)

Allegro

A one beat per measure pulse and light execution
will help propel this bright movement. It is elaborately
figured with Alberti bass, scales, thirds, and ornaments. Inventive use of either echo or terraced dynamics will enliven this <u>Allegro.</u>

      Length: 193 measures

      Technique: arpeggios, broken triads, double
         notes, ornaments, scales, Alberti bass,
         octaves, trills, broken octaves

Adagio (D Minor)

A slow arioso with many dramatic pauses, this
movement is difficult to unify. Tempo fluctuations are
the major hazard in this poignant <u>Adagio.</u>

      Length: 52 measures

      Technique: double notes, broken triads,
         ornaments, scales, arpeggios

Tempo di Menuet

This lively rondo-like movement builds power and excitement as it progresses. The two themes, one major and one minor, contrast effectively and lend themselves well to development. These variations consist of many lively figurations, including fast scales and arpeggios divided between the hands.

Length: 88 measures

Technique: ornaments, double notes, scales, arpeggios, various 16th-note figurations

SONATA, E Minor, Hob.XVI:34   <u>Early Advanced</u>
(ca. 1781/1782)

Presto

Compact and musically captivating, this movement is extremely accessible. Haydn's talent at its most subtle is apparent in this lyrical yet dramatic piece. Careful articulation is crucial for a unified concept of the work. Several contrapuntal lines occuring simultaneously comprise the most difficult aspect.

Length: 127 measures

Technique: broken triads, sustained and moving notes (contrapuntal lines), broken intervals, double notes

Adagio

A discursive and elaborate movement, this <u>Adagio</u> reveals a deep contemplative nature. The entire piece

should be performed with direction and sensitivity. Any technical problems are alleviated by the slow tempo.

Length: 49 measures

Technique: scales, broken intervals, arpeggios

Vivace molto (innocentemente)

The motivic and harmonic features are outstanding in this strong, driving rondo. It should be played robustly with subdued Alberti bass figures. This Finale closes an excellent and successful sonata.

Length: 136 measures

Technique: Alberti bass, scalar passages, turns

SONATA, C Major, Hob.XVI:35   Early Advanced
(ca. 1777/1779)

Allegro con Brio

Overwhelmingly popular, the technical and rhythmical problems in this charming sonata make it extremely difficult for an immature pianist to master. The ♩.♪ figure against a bass triplet and a three against four rhythm are major obstacles. When played effectively this movement is quite delightful.

Length: 170 measures

Technique: broken triads, awkward ornaments, 4 against 3, sustained and moving notes

Adagio (F Major)

This movement has very little character, with rather pedestrian melodies and harmonies. It opens much like the more successful slow movement of the Sonata in C, Hob. XVI/50.

> Length: 42 measures
> Technique: slow Alberti bass, scales,
>   ornaments, double 3rds

Finale

Many dotted rhythms and triplets animate this playful Rondo-like movement. The section in C minor adds a dramatic contrast. There are no major technical problems, though the piece requires a spirited and authoritative performance.

> Tempo: Presto
> Length: 97 measures
> Technique: double notes, sustained and moving
>   notes, L.H. scalar passages, broken octaves

SONATA, C# Minor, Hob.XVI:36   <u>Early Advanced</u>
(ca. 1777/79)

Moderato

A dramatic mood arises through the use of parallel octaves, sudden sforzandos, and pungent harmonies (including sequential diminished sevenths). Bravura figurations require manual dexterity.

> Length: 97 measures
> Technique: broken octaves, ornaments, broken
>   interval figurations, sustained and moving
>   notes, double notes, octaves, scales,
>   complex rhythms

Scherzando (A Major)

Although this piece is not as musically interesting as the previous movement, playful tunes and dotted figures render it pleasing and fun to play. It is an excellent scale etude. The "Scherzando" character should be emphasized.

> Tempo: Allegro con brio
> Length: 94 measures
> Technique: scales, double notes, ornaments

Menuet and Trio

The return to C# minor reiterates the rather somber mood of the opening movement. The Trio, in C# major, alleviates the tension. No major technical or rhythmic difficulties occur.

> Length: 55 measures
> Technique: scalar passages, octaves,
>   ornaments

SONATA, D Major, Hob.XVI:37   Early Advanced
    (ca. 1777/1779)

Allegro con Brio

Perhaps overly familiar, this movement is one of Haydn's most lovable and enjoyable. The work requires precise articulation and careful fingering. There are an abundance of innovative and intriguing harmonies. Difficult technical aspects include many sixteenth note figurations, fast ornaments, and arpeggios.

> Length: 103 measures
> Technique: 16th note figurations, scales,
>   arpeggios, fast ornaments, octaves,
>   double notes, sequential suspension

Largo e Sostenuto (D Minor)

    This <u>Largo</u> is a profound and effective contrast to the lighthearted gaiety of the outer movements. The pianist should heighten the expressive and rhythmic intensity. The movement concludes with "attacca subito il finale."

> Length: 19 measures
> Rhythm: various dotted rhythms, 32nd note
>   triplets, rolled chords, voicing

Finale

    Despite the sectional nature inherent in any rondo form, this piece is both coherent and cohesive. The variations on each theme will be even more effective if the pianist demarcates every articulation and dynamic subtlety. Emphasizing the occasional left hand melodies will add spark to this witty and boisterous finale.

> Tempo: Presto ma non troppo--
>   innocentemente
> Length: 123 measures
> Technique: trill figures, double notes, octaves,
>   16th note figurations

SONATA, Eb Major, Hob.XVI:38   <u>Early Advanced</u>
   (ca. 1777/1779)

Allegro Moderato

   A bright martial quality characterizes this brilliant
movement.   The thirty-second note scalar passages
require a proficient finger facility.
   Length: 76 measures
   Technique: scales, ornaments, double notes,
      rapid scalar passages, 32nd notes, sustained
      and moving notes, voicing, trills

Adagio (C Minor)

   The Adagio is propelled by a lilting Siciliano
rhythm.   Melodic and harmonic ingenuity creates a
haunting and beautiful air.   As with many of Haydn's
slow movements, this work is lyrical and expressive.
   Length: 45 measures
   Technique: arpeggios, fast two-note slurs,
      double notes, ornaments, trill figuration,
      cadenza-like runs

Finale

This movement is in the style of a brisk minuet, and is an unusual and intriguing ending to the sonata. The trio section in Ab provides an elegant contrast.

Tempo: Allegro
Length: 50 measures
Technique: octaves, double notes, ornaments

SONATA, G Major, Hob.XVI:39 <u>Advancing Intermediate</u>
(1780)

Allegro con Brio

Pleasant and amiable, this movement is an expanded version of the <u>Scherzando</u> in A Major from <u>Sonata,</u> Hob. XVI/36. A true "con brio" approach will emphasize the spirited and enjoyable qualities of this piece.

Length: 105 measures
Technique: broken intervals, scales, chromatic runs, ornaments, sustained and moving notes

Adagio (C Major)

A lengthy movement of considerable depth and scope, this work requires careful articulation of phrase shape. There are no technical difficulties which a slow tempo cannot obviate.

Length: 62 measures
Technique: arpeggios, scales, octaves, sustained and moving notes, scales in octaves, double 3rds

Prestissimo

This wonderfully exciting movement is the zenith of the sonata. It is not technically demanding and offers many opportunities for intelligent and creative use of dynamics, including terracing and echo effects.

Length: 121 measures
Technique: scales, broken triads, broken intervals, double notes, octaves

SONATA, G Major, Hob.XVI:40 Advancing Intermediate
(ca. 1782/1784)

Allegretto innocente

Varying the melodies either articulatively or dynamically will allay the monotony of this rather bland movement. The tempo should be determined by how fast the pianist can play the thirty-second notes, scales, and awkward ornaments.

Length: 100 measures
Technique: ornaments, double notes, scales, trill figures, chromatic runs, sustained and moving notes, 32nd note scales

Presto

This gay, rollicking rondo is captivating and should be played as briskly as possible. The rapid scales and passage work will provide good finger exercise. Rhythmic vitality and harmonic surprises characterize this example of Haydn's style at its most boisterous.

> Length: 82 measures
> Technique: scales, arpeggios, broken octaves,
> Alberti bass, ornaments, double notes,
> repeated notes and intervals

SONATA, Bb Major, Hob.XVI:41   Early Advanced
(ca. 1782/1784)

Allegro

Although the harmonies are compelling, the prosaic melodies make this a rather uneven work. Rhythmic precision is of the utmost importance. A combination of a faster tempo, creative dynamics, and interesting articulations would reveal the more engaging aspects of this Allegro.

> Length: 151 measures
> Technique: scales, fast trills, broken triads,
> sustained and moving notes, chromatic
> scalar passages

Allegro di Molto

An imitative <u>Allegro</u> containing elaborate counterpoint, this work is a fine example of Haydn's compositional skill.   The jovial theme gives the entire
movement a sprightly vitality. Haydn varies the theme
in inventive ways, making this piece a completely
satisfying musical experience.
>Length: 121 measures
>Technique: scales, double notes, broken triads,
>>broken intervals, sustained and moving
>>notes, hand independence

SONATA, D Major, Hob.XVI:42   Advanced
>(ca. 1782/1784)

Andante con Espressione

Though not as dark as many of Haydn's slow movements, this piece is introspective and contemplative.
The main obstacle is the rhythm, with seven different
rhythmic configurations in the first seven measures.
Subtle shaping of phrases is essential if the performer is
to project this beautiful theme and variations.
>Length: 105 measures
>Technique: double notes, chromatic runs,
>>scales, cadenza-like runs, ornaments,
>>complex rhythms

Vivace Assai

The contrapuntal nature of this delicate scherzo creates pianistic difficulties. In the imitative passages, skillful voicing is required. The entire sonata is very satisfying and enjoyable.

> Length: 101 measures
> Technique: broken intervals, scales, double
>   notes, sustained and moving notes

SONATA, Ab Major, Hob.XVI:43   <u>Early Advanced</u>
  (ca. 1771/1773)

Moderato

The delightful theme is the most attractive feature in this otherwise garrulous movement. Imaginative use of expressive devices may make this <u>Moderato</u> more interesting. The Alberti bass figures must be subdued.

> Length: 148 measures
> Technique: Alberti bass, scales, ornaments,
>   turns, 2 vs. 3, double 3rds, repeated notes

Menuet and Trio

While this <u>Menuet</u> has a quaint charm, the <u>Trio</u> is innocuous and banal. There are no major technical or rhythmic difficulties.

> Length: 40 measures
> Technique: double 3rds, Alberti bass

Rondo

The exciting <u>Rondo</u> is the redeeming feature of the sonata. It is frolicsome and vivacious and could be effectively performed by itself. Little or no musical interpretation is required in this sprightly movement.

> Tempo: Presto
> Length: 227 measures
> Technique: scales, arpeggios, broken intervals,
>   various figurations, sustained and moving
>   notes

SONATA, G Minor, Hob.XVI:44   <u>Early Advanced</u>
(ca. 1768/1770)

Moderato

There are rich, inventive harmonies, pungent appoggiaturas, and pregnant fermatas in this dramatic movement. Brilliant figuration permeates this poignant <u>Moderato.</u> Dynamics and careful shaping of every line are crucial.

> Length: 77 measures
> Technique: scales, ornaments, pedal point,
>   sustained and moving notes, broken chords

Allegretto

Somewhat lighter than the <u>Moderato</u>, this movement is still quite intense and profound. Challenging ornamentation is the only major difficulty. This rewarding sonata requires musical maturity.

> Length: 109 measures
> Technique: ornaments, scales, arpeggios,
> sustained and moving notes

SONATA, Eb Major, Hob.XVI:45 (1766)   <u>Early Advanced</u>

Moderato

Notable for the diversity of its many themes, this movement is an excellent example of Haydn's extremely personal use of the sonata/allegro structure. To implement the breezy grace of this work, a facile technique is essential.

> Length: 96 measures
> Technique: ornaments, trill-like figures,
> arpeggios, scales, Alberti bass, dotted
> rhythms, syncopation

Andante (Ab Major)

The poised elegance of this movement provides opportunities for subtle dynamic nuance. Each contrapuntal line needs accurate molding.

>Length: 73 measures
>Technique: scales, double 3rds, ornaments,
>   arpeggios, sustained and moving notes

Finale

In keeping with the character of this sonata, the Finale is joyfully and elegantly classical in style. The brilliant and ingratiating figurations are quite idiomatic, but require some dexterity.

>Tempo: Allegro di molto
>Length: 136 measures
>Technique: repeated notes, hand-crossings,
>   scales, broken triads, double 3rds, octaves

SONATA, Ab Major, Hob.XVI:46   Advanced
(ca. 1767/1768)

Allegro Moderato

Expansive and gleeful, this movement has numerous changes in color, texture, rhythm, and figuration. It is an interesting and challenging piece to play, but difficult to make cohesive. The figurations border on the realm of etude virtuosity.

> Length: 112 measures
> Technique: ornaments, scales, arpeggios,
>   complex rhythms, broken octaves, broken
>   intervals, double 3rds

Adagio (Db Major)

Technical and interpretive problems abound in this profoundly moving <u>Adagio</u>. The musical complexity is augmented by the numerous sections with two melodies in one hand and sustained and moving notes in the other. Intelligent phrasing and a smooth legato are of prime importance.

> Length: 80 measures
> Technique: double 3rds, ornaments (weak
>   finger), arpeggios, careful voicing,
>   sustained and moving notes

Finale

Harmonic cleverness and charm pervade this delightful <u>Finale</u>. A deft finger facility is the major requirement for performing this brilliant and light-hearted work.

> Tempo: Presto
> Length: 143 measures
> Technique: scales, broken intervals, various
>   fast figurations

SONATA, F Major, Hob.XVI:47   <u>Early Advanced</u>
   (before 1766)

Moderato

Legato scale passages are the principle feature of this <u>Moderato.</u>   It is not overwhelmingly beautiful or powerful, but with intelligent usage of articulations and dynamics, it can communicate impressively. The main technical problems are double thirds and octave scales.

> Length: 93 measures
> Technique: broken intervals, broken triads,
> double notes, ornaments, scales, arpeggios,
> octave scales

Larghetto (F Minor)

This exquisite <u>Larghetto</u> exists in exactly the same form, transposed to E Minor, as the first movement of the <u>Sonata in E Minor,</u> Cf. Hob. XVI/47. It is a poignant and wistful composition.

> Length: 47 measures
> Technique: scales, double notes, arpeggios,
> ornaments, appoggiaturas

Allegro

Because of its contrapuntal nature, this genial movement is a useful study in hand independence. Another version in the key of E Major serves as the second movement of the Sonata, Cf Hob. XVI: 47. This moderately difficult movement and its companions form a coherent and successful sonata.

> Length: 138 measures
>
> Technique: arpeggios, repeated notes, broken
>   intervals, scales, double notes, ornaments.

SONATA, E Minor, Cf.Hob.XVI:47   <u>Early Advanced</u>

Adagio

See Hob.XVI:47, 2nd movement.

Allegro

See Hob.XVI:47, 3rd movement.

Finale

Classically refined style and grace characterize this minuet-like movement. Dynamic and articulative nuance will enliven this light and elegant dance.

> Tempo: Tempo di menuet
> Length: 68 measures
> Technique: scales, ornaments, sustained
>   and moving notes

SONATA, C Major, Hob.XVI:48 (1789)   <u>Advanced</u>

Andante con Espressione

As with many of Haydn's mature slow movements, this theme and variations is very beautiful, and is almost romantic in its emotional depth. Careful counting is essential due to the many dotted rhythms, the slow tempo, and the variety of note values. The cadenza-like runs produce an improvisatory effect and must be played freely, yet within the beat.

> Length: 135 measures
> Technique: scales, arpeggios, chromatic runs,
>   ornaments, double notes, broken intervals,
>   complex rhythms

Rondo

The two movements of this sonata serve as effective foils as their differing characters complement each other perfectly. The tension built up in the Andante is dissipated in this dashing, rollicking piece. The many figurations require bravura.

> Tempo: Presto
> Length: 263 measures
> Technique: double notes, octave chords,
>   arpeggios, scales, broken intervals, sustained
>   and moving notes, octaves, ornaments

SONATA, Eb Major, Hob.XVI:49   Advanced
   (ca. 1789/1790)

Allegro

Mature and beautiful, this movement contains fermatas, constantly varying textures, off-beat accents, a short scalar cadenza, and rich chromatic harmonies-- characteristics of Haydn's later style. It is best suited to the sensitive pianist with fluent technique and good hand independence.

> Length: 218 measures
> Technique: double 3rds, scales, octaves, trills,
>   broken 3rds, Alberti bass, sustained and
>   moving notes, ornaments, hand-crossing,
>   cadenza

Adagio e Cantabile (Bb Major)

A wide spectrum of moods, figurations, and melodies make this one of Haydn's greatest slow movements.   Charm pervades the work, but passionate moments are skillfully interwoven to create a musical tapestry of profound expressivity.   Difficult articulations include two and three note slurs, portatos, and staccatos.   The sweep and intensity of the piece is heightened in the Bb minor middle section.

> Length: 124 measures
>
> Technique: scales, arpeggios, cadenza-like
>> figures, ornaments, broken intervals, Alberti bass, double notes, complex rhythms, hand-crossing

Finale

Though it may appear anti-climactic due to its brevity and simplicity, this winsome movement stabilizes the tremendous tension built up in the Adagio. Subduing the broken chord figures will allow the right hand triplets to soar.   A lyrical Eb minor middle section provides subtle contrast.

> Tempo: Tempo di Menuet
>
> Length: 115 measures
>
> Technique: double 3rds, scales, arpeggios,
>> 2 against 3, ornaments

SONATA, C Major, Hob.XVI:50   <u>Advanced</u>
   (ca. 1794/1795)

Allegro

This brilliant <u>Allegro</u> contains some of Haydn's most difficult music. It requires a sensitive and experienced pianist to articulate its wit and felicity. This movement is unique in that Haydn provides pedal markings for a mysterious veiled effect.

> Length: 150 measures
> Technique: double 3rd two-note slurs,
>   unusual pedalling, sustained and moving
>   notes, ornaments, broken octaves, scales,
>   chromatic runs, broken intervals, complex
>   rhythms, offbeat accents, careful voicing

Adagio (F Major)

Like many of Haydn's mature slow movements, this piece is deeply introspective. Its exquisite beauty is best expressed by a sensitive and accomplished pianist. Improvisational passages must be felt freely though still played within the beat. An earlier version of this movement is also included in the Landon Edition, Band 3.

> Length: 63 measures
> Technique: scales in octaves, sustained and
>   moving notes, cadenza-like runs, repeated
>   notes, arpeggios

Allegro Molto

Haydn's admirable sense of musical humor is illustrated in this movement. The pauses, the abrupt modulations to remote keys, and the boisterous good nature are all examples of the composer's wit. The instances of rolled chords in the right hand with sustained and moving notes in the left sound remarkably like Haydn's pieces for musical clock. This inventive Allegro closes one of Haydn's most brilliant and flamboyant sonatas.

> Length: 184 measures
> Technique: rolled chords, sustained and moving
>   notes, trill figures, double notes, repeated
>   notes, broken octaves

SONATA, D Major, Hob.XVI:51   Advanced
  (ca. 1794/1795)

Andante

Melodic octaves, double thirds, and rapid scales are the demanding technical features in this spirited movement. Haydn has substituted sheer tactile brilliance for profound depth of feeling, yet the work creates a lively and effective impression.

> Length: 111 measures
> Technique: grace notes, ornaments, arpeggios,
>   broken triads, scales in octaves, scales,
>   scalar passages in 3rds, double notes,
>   sustained and moving notes, various triplet
>   figurations, 4 against 3, 2 against 3

Finale

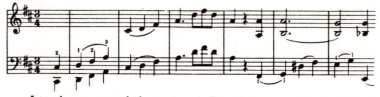

At times reminiscent of Beethoven, this brilliant scherzo-like movement contains suspensions, cross-rhythms and displaced accents, chromaticism, complex phrasing, and dense chordal texture.

> Tempo: Presto
> Length: 147 measures
> Technique: sustained and moving notes, double notes, arpeggios, scales, suspensions

SONATA, Eb Major, Hob.XVI/52 (1794)   Advanced

Allegro

Powerful declamation, charm, lyricism, and virtuosity combine here to create a masterwork. The movement is both technically and musically demanding and must be played with the utmost sensitivity. Problem sections contain fast double thirds, thirty-second notes, and contrapuntal complexities. A study of the marvelously creative harmonies and modulations would be invaluable.

> Length: 116 measures
> Technique: scales, runs, broken octaves, trill figures, double notes, complex rhythms, pedal point, octaves, 32nd note figuration, hand-crossing

Adagio (E Major)

Beautiful and profound, this movement in the unconventional and unexpected key of E Major requires both time and patience to fully explore its musical depths. Many double-dotted notes and changes of note value make this great work rhythmically complex. The cadenza-like figures should appear improvisatory, yet must be played in tempo. Special attention to difficult and widely varied articulations is essential.

> Length: 54 measures
> Technique: arpeggios (including diminished
>   7ths), scales, cadenza-like runs, grace notes,
>   ornaments, broken triads, double notes,
>   various dotted rhythms

Finale

Execution of this vigorous and challenging Presto requires fluent wrist movement in the repeated note figures. Observation of the fermatas will generate excitement. Tempo fluctuations are normal and predictable, and must be scrupulously avoided. An extraordinary sonata, this great work is one of Haydn's finest and most rewarding compositions.

> Tempo: Presto
> Length: 307 measures
> Technique: various figurations, broken triads,
>   arpeggios, scales, broken intervals, sustained
>   and moving notes, double notes

SONATA, D Major,   Advancing Intermediate
    Hob. XVII:D1 (before 1766)

Moderato—3 Variations

The theme is the sole varied aspect in this rather unassuming set of variations. The harmonies, bass line, and mode remain static. There are no rhythmic or technical problems.

> Length: 64 measures
> Technique: double notes, arpeggios, octaves,
>   constant RH figuration

Menuet

This simple <u>Menuet</u> without a trio is rather bland, but it has grace and melodic charm.

> Length: 16 measures
> Technique: ornaments, scalar passages

Finale

Lively and brilliant, this fast and amusing movement has many mordents. It is virtuosic with numerous scales, hand-crossings, and octaves, while remaining quite accessible. This work sounds more difficult than it actually is.

> Tempo: Allegro
> Length: 61 measures
> Technique: ornaments, scales, hand-crossings,
> octaves

SONATA, Eb Major, "No. 17,"   <u>Advancing Intermediate</u>
  without Hob. number (before 1766)

Moderato

Pompous, playful, and dramatic characters alternate throughout this movement. There are many complex rhythms and ornaments, of which trills are the most common.

> Length: 64 measures
> Technique: scales, runs, arpeggios,
> ornaments

Andante (C Minor)

This beautifully melodic and highly accessible movement is not rhythmically complex, allowing the pianist to concentrate on interpretive details. Each phrase should be carefully articulated.

> Length: 56 measures
> Technique: triplet broken chords, double
> thirds, ornaments

Menuetto and Trio

A few dramatic rests punctuate this rhythmic Minuet. The contrapuntal Trio is musical and harmonically innovative.

> Length: 50 measures
> Technique: arpeggios, double notes,
>   ornaments, sustained and moving notes

SONATA, Eb Major, "No.18,"   Early Advanced
   without Hob. number (before 1766)

Allegro

A clever development expands the main theme and introduces new material in this sonata/allegro. The tempo for the whole movement should be dictated by the difficult trills in measures 49-51.

> Length: 155 measures
> Technique: scales, leaps, 32nd note figuration,
>   octaves, ornaments, extended trills

Menuet and Trio

The gentle <u>Menuet</u> is contrasted with a more somber <u>Trio</u> in Eb minor, where syncopation adds interest. The overall mood is light and galant.

Length: 58 measures

Technique: scales

A TABLE OF NUMBERING SYSTEMS USED IN THE FIVE MOST READILY AVAILABLE EDITIONS OF THE SONATAS

The inconsistent numbering systems found in the many editions of Haydn's keyboard sonatas have been the source of much confusion. The following chart collates the numbers assigned to each sonata in the most prominent and readily available collections. The chart is based on the Hoboken catalogue, which is no longer accurate but still provides the most useful framework for comparing the various editions. The following editions have been utilized:

Joseph Haydn; Samtliche Klaviersonaten vol. 1, 2, and 3 (238, 240, 242). George Feder editor. G. Henle, 1972.

Joseph Haydn; 43 Piano Sonatas vol. 1 (1-11), 2 (12-33), 3 (24-33), and 4 (34-43), nr. 713 a, b, c, d. Kalmus Piano Series #3526, Belwin/Mills.

Joseph Haydn; 43 Piano Sonatas vol. 1 (1-11), 2 (12-23), 3 (24-33), and 4 (34-43). Carl Adolf Martienssen editor. C.F. Peters, 1937.

and...

Joseph Haydn; 6 leichten Divertimenti. Nr. 4443. Carl Adolf Martienssen editor. C.F. Peters, 1937.

Joseph Haydn; 20 Sonatas vol. 1 (1-10) and 2 (11-20) (Vol. 295, 196). Ludwig Klee and Sigmund Lebert editors. G. Schirmer, 1894.

Joseph Haydn; Samlitche Klaviersonaten vol. 1a (1-18), 1b (19-35), 2 (36-51), and 3 (52-62). UT 50026, 27, 28, 29. Christa Landon editor. Wiener Urtext (Universal), 1966.

A Note on the Editions

The Schirmer is totally antiquated and presents a limited number of sonatas in an over-edited form entirely inconsistent with current musicological and editorial practice. The fine Peters volumes (also reprinted by Kalmus) have now been superseded by the Wiener Urtext and Henle publications. Both of these editions are excellent and reveal the most scrupulous standards of contemporary scholarship. The Henle collection is the same editions as the Complete Edition of the Haydn Works, Series XVIII, vols. 1, 2, and 3. The Wiener Urtext edition attempts the most complete chronology of Haydn's sonatas, and the brilliant and copiously researched preface is indispensible to the serious student of Haydn's music.

Sonata	Key	Date	Henle	P.	S.	W.U.
Hob.XIV:5	D	1765/66	Vol.I 7 Sonaten 1765-1772 #4	x	x	28
(Fragment, W.V. Landon offers reconstruction.)						
Hob.XVI:1	C	before 1766	Vol.I Kleine Fruhe Sonaten #1	D1	x	10
Hob.XVI:G1	G	before 1766	Vol.I " #6	x	x	4
Hob.XVI:2	Bb	before 1766	Vol.I 9 Fruhe Sonaten #7	22	x	11
Hob.XVI:2a	d	before 1766	Vol.I Anhang 7 Verschollene #1	x	x	21
			Sonaten			
Hob.XVI:2b	A	before 1766	Vol.I " #2	x	x	22
Hob.XVI:2c	B	before 1766	Vol.I " #3	x	x	23
Hob.XVI:2d	Bb	before 1766	Vol.I " #4	x	x	24
Hob.XVI:2e	e	before 1766	Vol.I " #5	x	x	25
Hob.XVI:2g	C	before 1766	Vol.I " #6	x	x	26
Hob.XVI:2h	A	before 1766	Vol.I " #7	x	x	27
(Lost. Themes survive in Haydn's holograph "Entwurf-Katalog.")						
Hob.XVI:3	C	before 1766	Vol.I Kleine Fruhe Sonaten #8	D2	x	14
Hob.XVI:4	D	before 1766	Vol.I " #9	D3	x	9
Hob.XVI:5	A	before 1763	Vol.I 9 Fruhe Sonaten #2	23	x	8
(Authenticity doubtful.)						
Hob.XVI:6	G	before 1766	Vol.I 9 Fruhe Sonaten #6	37	x	13
Hob.XVI:7	C	before 1766	Vol.I Kleine Fruhe Sonaten #2	D5	x	2
Hob.XVI:8	G	before 1766	Vol.I " #3	D4	x	1
Hob.XVI:9	F	before 1766	Vol.I " #4	D6	x	3
Hob.XVI:10	C	before 1766	Vol.I " #7	43	x	6
Hob.XVI:11	G	?	Vol.I Anhang (mvts. 2 & 3)	11	x	5
(Doubtful version of Hob.XVI:G1)						
Hob.XVI:12	A	before 1766	Vol.I 9 Fruhe Sonaten #3	29	x	12
(Authenticity of first movement doubtful.)						
Hob.XVI:13	E	before 1766	Vol.I 9 Fruhe Sonaten #4	18	17	15
Hob.XVI:14	D	before 1766	Vol.I " #5	15	14	16
Hob.XVI:15	C	?	x	x	x	x
(Arrangement, not by Haydn, of Hob.XVI:11.)						
Hob.XVI:16	Eb	before 1766	Vol.I 9 Fruhe Sonaten #1	x	x	x
(Authenticity doubtful.)						

Sonata	Key	Date	Henle	P.	S.	W.U.
Hob.XVI:17	Bb	?	x	x	x	x
			(by Johann Gottfried Schwanberger)			
Hob.XVI:18	Bb	ca.1766/67	Vol.I 7 Sonaten #6	19	18	20
			1765-1772			
Hob.XVI:19	D	1767	Vol.I " #3	9	9	30
Hob.XVI:20	c	1771	Vol.II 6 Sonaten (b) #6	25	x	33
Hob.XVI:21	C	1773	Vol.II 6 Sonaten fur Furst #1	16	15	36
			Esterhazy			
Hob.XVI:22	E	?	Vol.II " #2	40	x	37
Hob.XVI:23	F	1773	Vol.II " #3	21	20	38
Hob.XVI:24	D	1773	Vol.II " #4	31	x	39
Hob.XVI:25	Eb	1773	Vol.II " #5	32	x	40
Hob.XVI:26	A	1773	Vol.II " #6	33	x	41
Hob.XVI:27	G	1776	Vol.II 6 Sonaten (a) #1	12	11	42
Hob.XVI:28	Eb	1776	Vol.II " #2	13	12	43
Hob.XVI:29	F	1774	Vol.II " #3	14	13	44
Hob.XVI:30	A	1776	Vol.II " #4	36	x	45
Hob.XVI:31	E	1776	Vol.II " #5	30	x	46
Hob.XVI:32	b	1776	Vol.II " #6	39	x	47
Hob.XVI:33	D	1771/73?	Vol.III 3 Sonaten #2	20	19	34
Hob.XVI:34	e	1771/73?	Vol.III " #3	2	2	53
Hob.XVI:35	C	1777/79?	Vol.II 6 Sonaten (b) #1	5	5	48
Hob.XVI:36	c#	1777/79?	Vol.II " #2	6	6	49
Hob.XVI:37	D	1777/79?	Vol.II " #3	7	7	50
Hob.XVI:38	Eb	1777/79?	Vol.II " #4	35	x	51
Hob.XVI:39	G	1780	Vol.II " #5	17	16	52
Hob.XVI:40	G	1782/84	Vol.III 3 Sonatas for #1	10	10	54
			Princessin Esterhazy			
Hob.XVI:41	Bb	1782/84	Vol.III " #2	27	x	55
Hob.XVI:42	D	1782/84	Vol.III " #3	28	x	56
Hob.XVI:43	Ab	1771/73?	Vol.III 3 Sonaten #1	41	x	35
Hob.XVI:44	g	1768/70?	Vol.I 7 Sonaten 1765-1772 #7	4	4	32
Hob.XVI:45	Eb	1766	Vol.I " #2	26	x	29
Hob.XVI:46	Ab	1767/68?	Vol.I " #5	8	8	31
Hob.XVI:47	F	after 1766	x	x	x	57
Hob.XVI:cf47	e	before 1766	Vol.I 7 Sonaten 1765-1772 #7	34	x	19
			(Two versions exist of this sonata. The version in F is			
			of a later date and probably not by Haydn.)			
Hob.XVI:48	C	1789	Vol.III 2 Sonaten 1789-1790 #1	24	x	58
Hob.XVI:49	Eb	1789/90	Vol.III " #2	3	3	59
Hob.XVI:50	C	1794/95	Vol.III 3 Englische Sonaten #2	42	x	60
Hob.XVI:51	D	1794/95	Vol.III " #3	38	x	61
Hob.XVI:52	Eb	1794	Vol.III " #1	1	1	62
Hob.XVI:D1	D	before 1766	Vol.I " #7	x	x	7
without Hob	Eb	before 1766	Vol.I 9 Fruhe Sonaten	x	x	17
without Hob	Eb	before 1766	Vol.I "	x	x	18
			(Authenticity doubtful. Early copy ascribed to "Marino			
			Romano Kayser" with different 3rd mvt. in Henle .)			

Note: In Peters, the "D" stands for "Divertimento."
H - Henle; P - Peters; S - Schirmer; W.U. - Wiener Urtext

III. AUTHENTIC TRANSCRIPTIONS

By the middle of the eighteenth century, the large and increasingly influential bourgeoisie had created a vast new demand for keyboard works for amateur use. This burgeoning market was supplied by a virtually inexhaustable flow of attractive and entertaining little miniatures, often in dance form. At the same time, composers created large quantities of dances for the ballrooms of an era noted for its lavish modes of social diversion. These works, intended for the private orchestras of a wealthy and privileged aristocracy, were often transcribed for the keyboard, providing the composer with doubled exposure and profit. The art of transcription was a common and aesthetically acceptable practice in the classical period, and it was through this medium that much of the music of the age was disseminated.

Among the innumerable transcriptions, arrangements, and variations on Haydn's dance movements and smaller occasional works, only a few may be credited to the composer himself with any certainty. Haydn's virtual isolation from the middle class audience until late in his life created little immediate need for the making of transcriptions, as the magnificence of the Esterhazy household insured a constant opportunity for the performance of orchestral dances. The authentic transcriptions that survive are almost without exception taken from sets made up of the two most popular dance forms of Haydn's age and environment—the German dance and the minuet. Characterized by clarity and rhythmic vitality, these generally simple and straightforward pieces are delightfully functional examples of their genre.

The earliest of these transcriptions is a group of Twelve Minuets, Hob.IX:3, probably dating from 1767, and originally composed for two violins, bass, flute, two oboes, and two horns. The manuscript of the version by Haydn of the Twelve Minuets Hob.IX:8 is preserved in the Esterhazy collections and derives from a set of orchestral dances no longer in existence. The Minuets and German Dances Hob.IX:11 and Hob.IX:12 were transcribed at the request of the Empress in December of 1792. Both works were originally scored for large orchestras of classical symphonic proportions, and were composed for the use of the imperial court. A setting of the famous anthem, "Gott! erhalte Franz den Kaiser," exists for piano, and current scholarship reveals that this version was made by the composer himself. "Gott! erhalte Franz den Kaiser" was composed during 1797 in response to the overwhelming impression produced by massed voices singing "God Save the King" which Haydn heard during his visits to England. On his return to Austria the composer presented his Emperor with this equally stirring patriotic Hymn. The familiar melody was incorporated into the famous "Emperor Quartet," Op. 76, No. 3, and the transcription of these variations long attributed to Gelinek may now be regarded as Haydn's own work.

The transcriptions Haydn made of his own works are typical examples of the composer's good humor and vital gaiety. Though generally sacrificing any particular depth of feeling for the less strenuous virtues of elegance and conviviality, these miniatures remain as fresh and engaging today as they were during Haydn's lifetime. Haydn's smaller dance forms may lack the rhythmic variety, assymetrical phrase structure, and harmonic ingenuity of his other, larger-scaled compositions, but many of these works possess a vigorous and refreshing charm.

Menueti (12 Minuets with 4 Trios) Hob.IX:3, 1-12 (1767)

MINUET AND TRIO, D Major, Hob.IX:3/1

Length: 44 measures

MINUET, G Major, Hob.IX:3/2

Length: 16 measures

MINUET, Bb Major, Hob.IX:3/3

Length: 16 measures

MINUET AND TRIO, F Major, Hob.IX:3/4

Length: 32 measures

MINUET AND TRIO, D Major,   Advancing Elementary
   Hob.IX:3/5, or "German Dance"

KRIEGER, Nana: Joseph Haydn--Little Dances for
   Young Folk (Universal-10270).

NOVIK, Ylda: Young Pianist's Guide to Haydn
(Studio P/R).
SHEALY, Alexander: Haydn--His Greatest Piano Solos
(Ashley).

This charming and remarkably pianistic piece is too
often overlooked. Occasional triplets and varying
dynamic levels add interest and spice. Fingering requires careful attention.
> Tempo: Allegro Con Brio
> Length: 40 measures
> Technique: octaves, double 3rds, leaps, trill

MINUET, Bb Major, Hob.IX:3/6

Length: 16 measures

MINUET AND TRIO, Eb Major　　Advancing Elementary
Hob.IX:3/7

KRIEGER, Nana: Joseph Haydn--Little Dances for
Young Folk (Universal-10270).
PACE, Robert: Music for Piano, Book 3
(Roberts/Schirmer) minuet only.
SHEALY, Alexander: Haydn--His Greatest Piano Solos
(Ashley).

The technical problems are easily solved in this
stately and enjoyable Minuet. Performers will find good

introductory work on two-note slurs. In the Trio, the right hand should bring out the melody and the left hand should be subdued.

Tempo: Allegro e risoluto
Length: 32 measures
Technique: double 3rds, leaps

MINUET, G Major, Hob.IX:3/8   Advancing Elementary

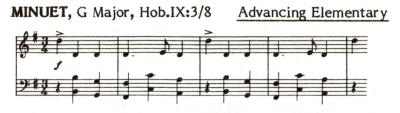

BRIMHALL, John: My First Book of Classics--Haydn
    (Hansen-H704).
HANSEN (Publisher): Joseph Haydn--A Highlight
    Collection...
KRIEGER, Nana: Joseph Haydn--Little Dances for
    Young Folk (Universal-10270).

To make this dull piece interesting, one pulse per measure should be felt. Almost constant octaves in the left hand are the only technical hurdle. Attention paid to dynamics and accents will also help.

Tempo: Moderato
Length: 16 measures
Technique: octaves

MINUET, C Major, Hob.IX:3/9

Length: 20 measures

MINUET, F Major, Hob.IX:3/10

Length: 24 measures

MINUET, C Major, Hob.IX:3/11

Length: 16 measures

MINUET, D Major, Hob.IX:3/12

Length: 20 measures

<u>**XII Menuets**</u> (12 minuets with 5 trios) Hob.IX:8, 1-12
(1785)

MINUET AND TRIO, C Major,   <u>Early Intermediate</u>
   Hob.IX:8/1

ALFRED (Publisher): Haydn—15 of his Easiest...

ANSON, George: Anson Introduces Haydn--German Dances (Willis).

CLARK and GOSS: Piano Literature...Book 5a, Book 5a-6a (Summy-Birchard).

ETTS, May L.: Beginning to Play Haydn (Schroeder & Gunther).

HEINRICHSHOFEN (Publisher): Haydn--Easier Favorites, Urtext (Peters #4049).

HUGHES, Edwin: Haydn--Master Series for the Young (G. Schirmer).

KRIEGER, Nana: Joseph Haydn--Little Dances for Young Folk (Universal-10270).

LANNING, Russell: Music by the Masters (Musicord/Belwin-Mills).

MOTCHANE, Marthe Morhange: An Introduction to Pianistic Styles, Book 2, Classical (Bourne).

NOVIK, Ylda: Young Pianist's Guide to Haydn (Studio P/R).

SCHOLZ, Erwin Christian: Music for the Home With Joseph Haydn (Bosworth) minuet only.

SHEALY, Alexander: Haydn--His Greatest Piano Solos (Ashley).

Both melodically and harmonically engaging, this lengthy Minuet and Trio is notable for both its scope and quality. The only difficulties are sustained and moving notes in the left hand and extended two against three passages. Rhythm, notes, and dynamics vary among editions. Once learned, this joyful piece would be a successful and enjoyable recital selection.

> Tempo: Allegro
> Length: 48 measures
> Technique: sustained and moving notes in L.H., 2 against 3

MINUET, A Major, Hob.IX:8/6   <u>Advancing Elementary</u>

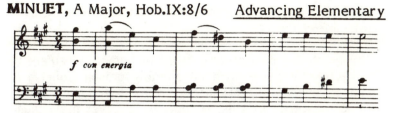

BRIMHALL, John: My First Book of Classics--Haydn
    (Hansen-H704).
HANSEN (Publisher): Joseph Haydn--A Highlight
    Collection...
KRIEGER, Nana: Joseph Haydn--Little Dances for
    Young Folk (Universal-10270).
SHEALY, Alexander: Haydn--His Greatest Piano Solos
    (Ashley).
SZAVAI, Veszpremi: Klaviermuzik, No. 1
    (Musica Budapest/Belwin-Mills).

This charming and energetic <u>Minuet</u> is one of
Haydn's most interesting, with daring harmonies and
"horn fifths."   It is accessible to the less advanced
performer who can reach an octave.   An effective
recital program might combine this engaging piece with
one or two other dances.
        Tempo: Moderato
        Length: 16 measures
        Technique: double notes, octaves, grace notes,
            sudden register changes

MINUET AND TRIO, D Major,   <u>Advancing Elementary</u>
        Hob.IX:8/7

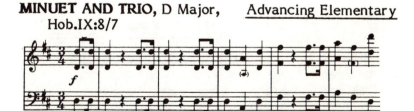

KRIEGER, Nana: Joseph Haydn--Little Dances for
    Young Folk (Universal-10270).

SHEALY, Alexander: Haydn--His Greatest Piano Solos
(Ashley).

Haydn's famous musical sense of humor is evident in
this delightful piece with an opening unison flourish in
three octaves.   Unfortunately, while the double thirds
can be mastered at this tempo, the octaves may cause
problems for small hands.   Surmounting the technical
difficulties is well worth the effort.   Careful attention
to dynamics and articulations will reveal the martial
character of this work.

Tempo: Allegro maestoso
Length: 44 measures
Technique: octaves, double 3rds, ornaments

MINUET, G Major, Hob.IX:8/8

Length: 16 Measures

MINUET, E Major, Hob.IX:8/9,   <u>Early Intermediate</u>
or "Country Dance"

BRIMHALL, John: My First Book of Classics--Haydn
(Hansen-H704).
CLARK and GOSS: Piano Literature...Book 4a
(Summy-Birchard).
HANSEN (Publisher): Joseph Haydn--A Highlight
Collection...
KRIEGER, Nana: Joseph Haydn--Little Dances for
Young Folk (Universal-10270).

OLSON, BIANCHI, BLICKENSTAFF: Repertoire 4B
    (C. Fischer).
SHEALY, Alexander: Haydn--His Greatest Piano Solos
    (Ashley).

This straightforward <u>Minuet</u> is considerably more demanding than it appears. The right hand octaves that outline triads are quite difficult, as are the triplets and the ornaments. The Clark and Goss and the Olson, Bianchi, and Blickenstaff editions divide these octaves between the hands.

> Tempo: Allegro vivace e risoluto
> Length: 16 measures
> Technique: double notes (octaves), ornaments,
> triplet runs, trills

MINUET AND TRIO, C Major,   Advancing Elementary
    Hob.IX:8/10

ANSON, George: Anson Introduces Haydn--German
    Dances (Willis).
HEINRICHSHOFEN (Publisher): Haydn--Easier
    Favorites, Urtext (Peters #4049).
KRIEGER, Nana: Joseph Haydn--Little Dances for
    Young Folk (Universal-10270).
NOVIK, Ylda: Young Pianist's Guide to Haydn
    (Studio P/R).
SHEALY, Alexander: Haydn--His Greatest Piano Solos
    (Ashley).
WELCH, John: Schroeder's Favorite Classics, Vol. I
    (Studio P/R).

This excellent performance piece, with a delicate <u>Trio</u> in C Minor, lends itself to imaginative and creative use of articulations and dynamics. The double thirds and sixths are quite challenging. Novik and Heinrichshofen alleviate this problem by either dividing these passages between the hands or leaving out the optional lower note entirely.

> Tempo: Allegro giocoso
> Length: 40 measures
> Technique: double 3rds and 6ths, varied
>   touches

MINUET, G Major, Hob.IX:8/11

Length: 58 measures

MINUET, F Major, Hob.IX:8/12, or   Elementary
    "Little Dance," "Little Serenade," "German Dance"

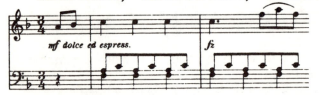

AGAY, Denes: The Joy of Classics (Yorktown).
ANSON, George: Anson Introduces Haydn--German
    Dances (Willis).
ANTHONY, George W.: Purcell to Mozart--Easy, Vol. 1
    (Presser).
BASTIEN, James: Easy Piano Classics (Kjos West).
BRIMHALL, John: My First Book of Classics--Haydn
    (Hansen-H704).
ETTS, May L.: Beginning to Play Haydn
    (Schroeder & Gunther).
FREY, Martin: The New Sonatina Book
    (Schott Ed. 2891 AP).

KRIEGER, Nana: Joseph Haydn—Little Dances for
Young Folk (Universal-10270).
LANNING, Russell: Music by the Masters
(Musicord/Belwin-Mills).
SHEALY, Alexander: Haydn—His Greatest Piano Solos
(Ashley).
WEITZMANN, Fritz: Haydn—Easiest Piano Pieces
(Peters No. 5004).

This pianistic yet simple piece is made up of pleasing melodies. Much can be done with the two-note slurs (some editions leave these out, but they can easily be added by the pupil or teacher). Two simple trills give the elementary pianist an opportunity to learn this technique.

> Tempo: Allegretto
> Length: 20 measures
> Technique: trills, sustained and moving notes
> in L.H.

Menuetti di ballo (12 neue Redout Menuette)
(12 minuets with 11 trios) Hob.IX:11, 1-12 (1792)

MINUET AND TRIO, D Major, Hob.IX:11/1

Length: 48 measures

MINUET AND TRIO, Bb Major, Hob.IX:11/2

Length: 32 measures

MINUET AND TRIO, G Major,   Early Intermediate
Hob.IX:11/3, or "German Dance"

AGAY, Denes: Classics to Moderns, Vol. 37
(Consolidated).
AMSCO (Publisher): It's Easy to Play Classics.

The effective exchange of motives between hands
provides good practice for finger and hand independence
in this lively transcription.   When the left hand has
accompaniment figures, they should be subdued, and the
right hand should sing out.   Effective dynamics and
articulations will add vigor.
          Tempo: Allegro Con Brio
          Length: 40 measures
          Technique: scales, arpeggios, sustained and
              moving notes, double 3rds, 2 against 3,
              tricky transitions from triplets to 8th notes

MINUET, E Minor   Advancing Elementary
Hob.IX:11/4 (Trio), or "German Dance"

AGAY, Denes: The Joy of Recital Time (Yorktown)
trio only.

This spirited piece is quite accessible and fun to
play.   For extra sparkle, the articulations should be
highlighted.   The ornamental figures to be played on the
beat may prove a problem.

Tempo: Allegretto
Length: 16 measures
Technique: scalar passages, ornaments, octave
jumps

MINUET AND TRIO, C Major, Hob.IX:11/5

Length: 32 measures

MINUET AND TRIO, F Major, Hob.IX:11/6

Length: 44 measures

MINUET AND TRIO, D Major, Hob.IX:11/7

Length: 44 measures

MINUET AND TRIO, Eb Major, Hob.IX:11/8

Length: 32 measures

MINUET AND TRIO, C Major, Hob.IX:11/9

Length: 36 measures

MINUET, G Major, Hob.IX:11/10

Length: 16 measures

MINUET AND TRIO, Eb Major, Hob.IX:11/11

Length: 36 measures

MINUET AND TRIO, D Major, Hob.IX:11/12

Length: 40 measures

XII neue deutche Tanze (12 German Dances with trio
and coda) Hob.IX:12, 1-12 (1792)

Note: All of the German Dances Hob.IX:12 are in:

ZEITLIN and GOLDBERGER: F.J. Haydn--A Digest of
Short Piano Works (Boston-13789).

Other sources are listed with each composition.

GERMAN DANCE, G Major,   Advancing Elementary
Hob.IX:12/1

BARRATT, Carol: Chester's Concert Pieces, Vol. 2
(Chester).

This simple yet elegant German dance is well within
the realm of the elementary pianist's ability, providing
an opportunity to work on dynamics and articulation.
There are no technical difficulties, especially if fingerings are carefully noted. Combined with other German
dances, it would be good for recitals.

> Tempo: Allegretto
> Length: 16 measures
> Technique: pedal point, double 3rds, sustained
>   and moving notes

GERMAN DANCE, Bb Major, Hob.IX:12/2   <u>Elementary</u>

CLARK and GOSS: Piano Literature...Book 3
   (Summy-Birchard).

Although challenging, the technique in this piece is within the grasp of the elementary student. Careful attention to fingering is important. This pleasant transcription would be excellent for performance if paired with one or two other Haydn dances.
   Tempo: Moderato con moto
   Length: 16 measures
   Technique: scalar passages, appoggiaturas,
      sustained and moving notes

GERMAN DANCE, G Major,   <u>Advancing Elementary</u>
   Hob.IX:12/3

CLARK and GOSS: Piano Literature...Book 3
   (Summy-Birchard).

The elegance and grace of the classical period are exemplefied in this simple little piece. It is an excellent study for left hand independence. Paired with another dance, this would go well on a recital program.
   Tempo: Allegretto
   Length: 16 measures
   Technique: sustained and moving notes, 3rds,
      scales, grace notes

GERMAN DANCE, C Major,   <u>Advancing Elementary</u>
   Hob.IX:12/4 (with Trio)

AGAY, Denes: From Bach to Bartok, Vol. C (Warner).
BARRATT, Carol: Chester's Concert Pieces, Vol. 2
   (Chester).
NOVIK, Ylda: Young Pianist's Guide to Haydn
   (Studio P/R).
WEITZMANN, Fritz: Haydn--Easiest Piano Pieces
   (Peters No. 5004).

    Elegance and harmonic invention characterize this
piece. The articulations and ornaments require imaginative treatment. The double thirds in both hands at the
beginning create a beautiful effect if the hands are
perfectly synchronized. The <u>Trio</u> is delightful and
creates a humorous effect by the use of sforzandi.
       Tempo: Moderato
       Length: 32 measures
       Technique: double 3rds, scalar passages

GERMAN DANCE, G Major,   <u>Advancing Elementary</u>
   Hob.IX:12/5

ANSON, George: Anson Introduces Haydn--German
   Dances (Willis).

    Attention should be paid to dynamics and articula-
tions to highlight the boisterous qualities of this dance.
Left hand accompaniment chords should be subdued in

the first section. The second section is fun to play.
>Tempo: Allegretto
>Length: 16 measures
>Technique: sustained and moving notes in RH,
>pedal point

GERMAN DANCE, D Major,   Advancing Elementary
>Hob.IX:12/6

This German Dance is very charming. If fingering is
carefully observed, technical problems will be avoided.
The sustained and moving note octave figure in the
accompaniment may be difficult for the pianist with
small hands. The sf diminished seventh chord requires
preparation.
>Tempo: Andante
>Length: 16 measures
>Technique: octaves, double notes in L.H.,
>scalar figures

GERMAN DANCE, G Major,   Advancing Elementary
>Hob.IX:12/7

ANSON, George: Anson Introduces Haydn--German
>Dances (Willis).
CLARK and GOSS: Piano Literature...Book 2
>(Summy-Birchard).
OLSON, BIANCHI, BLICKENSTAFF: Repertoire 4B
>(C. Fischer).

This rather static <u>German Dance</u> contains some unusual dissonances. There are difficult reaches, large leaps (up a 10th and down a 12th), and awkward finger positions. The various editions present conflicting articulations.

> Tempo: Allegretto
> Length: 16 measures
> Technique: large leaps

GERMAN DANCE, D Major, <u>Advancing Elementary</u>
Hob.IX:12/8

This pleasant piece would be an excellent scale and pentachord study for the right hand. The melody is made up entirely of either octaves or scalar figures. The pianist should attempt to bring out the subtle dynamic nuances to increase the vitality of this delightful recital piece.

> Tempo: Vivace
> Length: 20 measures
> Technique: octaves, scales, pentachords

GERMAN DANCE, Bb Major, <u>Advancing Elementary</u>
Hob.IX:12/9

This refreshing miniature is lovely and accessible. The only trouble spot is in the fourth measure, with right hand scalar double thirds.

Tempo: Allegro
Length: 16 measures
Technique: double 3rds, chords, scalar
passages

GERMAN DANCE, C Major,   Advancing Elementary
Hob.IX:12/10

AGAY, Denes: More Easy Classics to Moderns, Vol. 27
(Consolidated).

ANSON, George: Anson Introduces Haydn--German
Dances (Willis).

BRIMHALL, John: My First Book of Classics--Haydn
(Hansen-H704).

CLARK and GOSS: Piano Literature...Book 3,
Books 3-4a-4b (Summy-Birchard).

ETTS, May L.: Beginning to Play Haydn
(Schroeder & Gunther).

GRANT, Lawrence: Piano Music by the Great Masters
(Ashley).

OZANIAN, Carole: Piano Album, Level 1a
(Studio P/R).

WEITZMANN, Fritz: Haydn--Easiest Piano Pieces
(Peters No. 5004).

The pianist should learn the more difficult second
half first.   Careful fingering and balance of hands is
important.   Effective dynamic control will create an
interesting piece for performance.

Tempo: Moderato (Allegretto)
Length: 16 measures
Technique: arpeggiated passages in RH, pedal
point, sustained and moving notes

GERMAN DANCE, F Major,   <u>Advancing Elementary</u>
    Hob.IX:12/11

BRIMHALL, John: My First Book of Classics--Haydn
    (Hansen-H704).

The beautiful melodies in this dance provide the performer with an excellent opportunity to learn correct accentuation. The opening octaves are the only technical problem. Care should be taken to subdue the left hand accompaniment.
        Tempo: Allegretto
        Length: 16 measures
        Technique: octaves, scales

GERMAN DANCE, D Major,   <u>Advancing Elementary</u>
    Hob.IX:12/12 (with Coda)

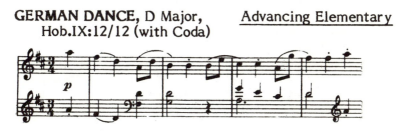

ANSON, George: Anson Introduces Haydn--German
    Dances (Willis).
BRIMHALL, John: My First Book of Classics--Haydn
    (Hansen-H704).

This wonderful <u>German Dance</u> has lovely melodies and interesting harmonies. Technically, the piece is not demanding. Many sections offer an opportunity for creative articulations and dynamics. The lengthy coda provides a brilliant conclusion to this fine group of German Dances. A selection from this set would supply attractive and unfamiliar recital fare.

Tempo: Allegro
Length: 36 measures
Technique: double 3rds, broken octaves, 16th
note octave tremolo, broken chords

Gott! erhalte Franz den Kaiser   <u>Early Intermediate</u>
(National Anthem) Hob. XXVIa:43 (1797)

WEITZMANN, Fritz: Haydn--Easiest Piano Pieces
(Peters No. 5004).

Excellent exercise in voicing and playing chordal
music is found here, as well as an introduction to pedalling. The pianist should be able to hear and bring out
the familiar melody when working on voicing.

Tempo: Langsam (slowly)
Length: 16 measures
Technique: melody in double notes, chords,
sustained and moving notes

IV. TRANSCRIPTIONS FROM OTHER MEDIA

In the closing decades of the eighteenth century, the piano had become the favorite instrument for home music making, and the many amateur pianists demanded short and technically easy works of a light and entertaining nature. Transcriptions of familiar symphonic and chamber works were an essential element of this rapidly expanding market. Haydn's position as one of the first composers to achieve true international celebrity insured that the most engaging and diverting of his larger compositions would quickly reach the public in simple, condensed piano versions. In an era in which copyright laws were nonexistent, publishers across Europe were eager to release transcriptions (often by anonymous copyists) of Haydn's extremely popular works. During the classical period, transcription did not bear the stigma of aesthetic bastardization it does today, and Haydn proved his own willingness to make arrangements for piano and musical clock of his larger works. Though not authentic Haydn, the many transcriptions of his best known compositions are completely in keeping with eighteenth century artistic practice. Many of these arrangements are quite delightful, have a proven pedagogical value, and are firmly and rightly established as part of the pianist's repertoire.

Haydn's fame reached its zenith during his last years and, as a result, the mass of transcriptions are primarily taken from his mature compositions. The majority derive from the ever-popular symphonies, though the string quartets also provided much adaptable material. The well-known "Twelve Short Pieces for Piano" and the delightful "La Roxelaine" have occupied an important position throughout two centuries. Haydn's original piano music contains virtually nothing suitable for the beginning pianist, and as a result many easy transcriptions are made, even today, in an effort to make one of the foremost composers in the history of western music accessible to an expanding group of young musicians. Through the medium of transcription, it has become possible for many of the characteristic and salient features of Haydn's music to be effectively communicated to the largest potential audience.

ANDANTE or ALLEGRETTO,   Early Intermediate
    A Major (from Symphony Hob.I:53/2, "L'Imperiale")

ETTS, May L.: Beginning to Play Haydn
    (Schroeder & Gunther).
PACE, Robert: Music for Piano, Book 6
    (Roberts/Schirmer).
WEITZMANN, Fritz: Haydn--Easiest Piano Pieces
    (Peters No. 5004).

This curious piece exists in two completely divergent forms. Weitzmann presents a more plausible copy of the work in the form of a theme and two variations, one of which is in the minor. This variation has been printed separately in the Etts edition. The textures and figurations are closely related to Haydn. Pace and Etts provide identical copies of a much more elaborate work (at an advancing intermediate level) with fast arpeggios and chromatic figurations. Several of the arpeggios exceed the range of Haydn's keyboard, and the figurations are more reminiscent of the romantic era than the classical period. The more representative and less difficult Weitzmann edition is recommended.

Length: 64 measures
Technique: scales, arpeggios, double notes in
    L.H., Alberti bass

LA ROXELAINE, Air with Variations,   Intermediate
C Minor (from Symphony Hob.I:63/2)

HUGHES, Edwin: Haydn--Master Series for the Young
(G. Schirmer).
KALMUS #3534: Haydn--Eight Various Compositions
(Belwin-Mills).
PHILIPP, Isadore: Joseph Haydn--Huit Pieces
(Durand Nr. 11592).
SHEALY, Alexander: Haydn--His Greatest Piano Solos
(Ashley).
ZEITLIN and GOLDBERGER: F.J. Haydn--A Digest of
Short Piano Works (Boston-13789).

With any transcription, especially a symphonic one
such as this, it is recommended that the pianist become
familiar with the original orchestral version to get the
proper flavor and color. An unusual feature of this work
is the constant alternation of major and minor variations. Double notes, particularly thirds, are the primary
technical problems in variations I, III, and V. Other
difficulties are easily overcome. This charming and
challenging set will be quite successful if the pianist
pays careful attention to the articulations and dynamics, perhaps even exaggerating them. The piece has
been in print as a piano solo since late in Haydn's life,
though it is no longer considered to have been transcribed by him.
                    Tempo: Allegretto
                    Length: 127 measures
                    Technique: scales, arpeggios, broken 3rds,
                        double notes (3rds, 6ths, octaves), chords,
                        large reaches, repeated notes

MINUET AND TRIO, Eb Major   <u>Intermediate</u>
(from Symphony Hob.I:76/3)

WEITZMANN, Fritz: Haydn--Easiest Piano Pieces
(Peters No. 5004).

This good-natured piece provides an enjoyable study in articulation. Most of these are notated, but experimentation is encouraged. To emphasize the lively character, one pulse per measure should be felt. Paired with another dance this would be a pleasant recital selection.

Tempo: Allegro
Length: 50 measures
Technique: octaves, double notes

MINUET AND TRIO, Bb Major   <u>Advancing Elementary</u>
(from Symphony Hob.I:77/3)

GLOVER, David Carr: Piano Student, Level 6
(Belwin-Mills).
MIROVITCH, Alfred: Introduction to Piano Classics
(G. Schirmer).

Idiomatic figuration and unusual phrase shape characterize this boisterous <u>Minuet</u>. The straightforward rhythmic drive will make a direct appeal to the younger player.

Tempo: Allegretto
Length: 45 measures
Technique: scales, arpeggios, chords, octaves,
double 3rds, sudden dynamic changes

GERMAN DANCE, G Major <u>Elementary</u>
(from Symphony Hob.I:81/3 (trio))

AGAY, Denes: From Bach to Bartok, Vol. B (Warner).
OLSON, Lynn Freeman: Exploring More Piano
Literature (C. Fischer).

A Moderato tempo with eighth note scalar passages
make this cheerful <u>German Dance</u> a good etude in scale
technique.   However, the constant left hand intervals
and chords could sound thumpy and monotonous.
Tempo: Moderato, ben ritmo (Allegretto)
Length: 24 measures
Technique: scalar passages

ROMANCE, F Major <u>Advancing Elementary</u>
(from Symphony Hob.I:82/2 "L'Ours")

RUTHARDT, Adolf: Easy Sonatinas and Short Recital
Pieces, Vol. II (Peters #3195b).

This piece is not difficult and has melodic and harmonic interest.   It would be a good musical exercise for
the less experienced pianist. Ruthardt gives an editorial

suggestion as to how to play the tricky turns.

> Tempo: Moderato assai
> Length: 32 measures
> Technique: ornaments, turns, double 3rds

RONDO, Bb Major,   Advancing Elementary
     (from Symphony Hob.I:85/4, "La Reine")

MOTCHANE, Marthe Morhange: An Introduction to
     Pianistic Style, Book 2, Classical (Bourne).

Haydn's charming and witty style is found in this
wonderfully pianistic transcription. The lyrical possibilities of each contrapuntal line should be explored. The
technical aspects aren't a problem, even at a fast
tempo. This would be an excellent recital choice.

> Tempo: Presto
> Length: 24 measures
> Technique: scalar passages, double 3rds,
>   octave leaps

FINALE, G Major   Advancing Elementary
     (from Symphony Hob.I:88/4, adapted by
      M. Clementi)

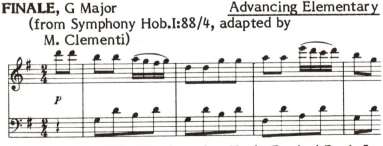

PALMER and LETHCO: Creating Music Recital Book 5
     (Alfred).

Buoyant and dramatic, this well-known and engaging theme is not difficult. It should be played lightly, taking note to bring out contrapuntal lines, dynamics, and articulations.

        Tempo: Allegro con spirito
        Length: 32 measures
        Technique: Alberti bass, double 3rds

MENUETTO AND TRIO, G Major   <u>Early Intermediate</u>
   (from Symphony Hob.I:94/3, "Surprise")

ALFRED (Publisher): Haydn--15 of his Easiest...
WEYBRIGHT, June: Course for Pianists, Book Five
   (Belwin-Mills).

Unfortunately, this wonderful piece loses much in transcription. The performer should attempt to capture the charm and elegance of the orchestral version. As with nearly any transcription, the inner voices provide excellent work for hand independence.

        Tempo: Allegro
        Length: 90 measures
        Technique: broken octaves, arpeggios, scales,
           sustained and moving notes, appoggiaturas

MINUET, C Minor   <u>Early Intermediate</u>
   (from Symphony Hob.I:95/3)

AGAY, Denes: Classics to Moderns, Intermediate,
    Vol. 37 (Consolidated).
GRANT, Lawrence: More Classic to Contemporary
    Music (Ashley).

The large scope of this <u>Minuet</u> makes it pianistic
and intriguing to play.   There are various articulations
as well as a few contrapuntal lines.   Paired with another
minuet, perhaps one in a major key, this work would be
good for a recital.   The difficulties can be overcome at
a slower tempo.
    Tempo: Allegretto
    Length: 55 measures
    Technique: sustained and moving notes,
        octaves, wide skips, grace notes

MINUET, C Major   Elementary
    (from Symphony Hob.I:97/3)

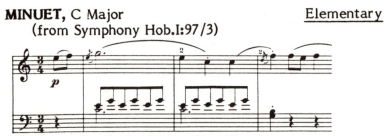

ETTS, May L.: Beginning to Play Haydn
    (Schroeder & Gunther).

Although there is little melodic variety, this piece
is easily accessible to the elementary pianist who would
enjoy the easy and effective ornaments.   Sustained and
moving notes are the major difficulty in this harmonically simple, yet attractive, piece.
    Tempo: Moderato
    Length: 24 measures
    Technique: sustained and moving notes,
        broken 3rds, ornaments

MINUET, G Major   Early Intermediate
(from Symphony Hob.I:100/3, "Military")

CASTLE, Joseph: Mel Bay's Student Piano Classics--
  Haydn (Mel Bay-63069).
NIKOLAEV, A.: The Russian School of Piano Playing,
  Book II (Boosey & Hawkes).

Once this jolly piece is learned, it will prove very
amusing. The sixteenth-note upbeats add rhythmic
impetus. Care should be taken to play these figures as
evenly as possible. In the second section, the left hand
has the main melody while the right has a little counter-
melody. The Castle version is somewhat easier.
          Tempo: Moderato
          Length: 28 measures
          Technique: scales, chords, double notes,
            sustained and moving notes

ALLEGRETTO, Eb Major,   Advancing Elementary
(from Overture Hob.Ia:15/2, from the Opera
  "La Vera Constanza," Hob.XXVIII:8) (Op.46, No.6)

ROYAL CONSERVATORY OF MUSIC, Grade IV
  (Frederick Harris).

This charming little piece exemplifies Haydn's good-
natured musical wit. The sixteenth-note passages are
somewhat difficult but can be learned at a slower
tempo. Correct fingerings are important and will aid

the initial study. The performer should be able to hear each contrapuntal line in the second section. Careful attention to dynamics will bring out the humorous elements. This would be enjoyable as a recital selection.

> Length: 44 measures
> Technique: hand-crossing, scales, arpeggios

MINUET AND TRIO, C Major   Advancing Elementary
(from Divertimento Hob.II:11/3, "Mann und Weib")

AGAY, Denes: Sonatinas, Vol. A (Warner) trio only.
ANSON, George: Anson Introduces Haydn--German
    Dances (Willis) trio only.
BASTIEN, James: Easy Piano Classics (Kjos West)
    trio only.
BASTIEN, James: First Piano Repertoire Album
    (Kjos West) trio only.
BRADLEY, Richard: Big Note Teaching Pieces...Vol. 1
    (Bradley) trio only.
ETTS, May L.: Beginning to Play Haydn
    (Schroeder & Gunther) trio only.
SZAVAI-VESPREMI: Album for Piano, No. 1
    (Belwin-Mills) minuet only.

This unusual Minuet has an attractive two-voice structure. The consistent counterpoint will give the advancing elementary pianist an opportunity to work on playing two independent lines at once. The fascinating phrase structure is rather irregular, and there are amusing echo effects. The tempo should be stately, in the baroque manner. It is not difficult and would make a nice recital selection. The charming Trio, often published separately, is one of Haydn's most familiar pieces.

Tempo: Allegretto
Length: 28 measures
Technique: arpeggios, scales

AIR AND FIVE VARIATIONS, C Major <u>Intermediate</u>
(from Divertimento Hob.II:11/4, "Mann und Weib")

AGAY, Denes: From Bach to Bartok, Vol. A (Warner)
    theme only.
ANTHONY, George W.: Purcell to Mozart--Easy, Vol. 1
    (Presser).
ETTS, May L.: Beginning to Play Haydn
    (Schroeder & Gunther) theme.
HEINRICHSHOFEN (Publisher): Haydn--Easier
    Favorites, Urtext (Peters #4049).

Lovely and galant, this piece is an excellent introduction to Haydn's larger keyboard works. The simple
theme, while not especially interesting harmonically, is
melodically very beautiful. Variation I embellishes the
theme with scales and a two-note slur figure using
repeated notes. Variation III is ornamented almost
entirely with fast runs. This variation may seem difficult, but the five or six note scales can be played easily
once learned. Variation IV is probably the trickiest due
to leaps and leger lines. The left hand is embellished in
variation V. This piece is highly recommended for
performance.

Tempo: Moderato
Length: 96 measures
Technique: scales, repeated notes, leaps

MINUET, Eb Major   Advancing Intermediate
   (from String Quartet Hob.III:38/2)

CLARK and GOSS: Piano Literature...Book 5a and
   Book 5a-6a (Summy-Birchard).

Though rather difficult, this charming and clever
piece is well worth the effort required to learn it. The
consistent counterpoint is good for hand independence.
The pianist should emphasize voicing, and fingerings
should be noted carefully to aid in the learning process. This brilliant <u>Minuet</u> is recommended for recital
use.

> Tempo: Allegretto
> Length: 68 measures
> Technique: leaps, arpeggios, scales, scales
>   in 6ths and 3rds, double notes, Alberti bass

ALLEGRETTO, G Major   Early Intermediate
   (from String Quartet Hob.III:41/4)

WEITZMANN, Fritz: Haydn--Easiest Piano Pieces
   (Peters No. 5004).

The major difficulties in this lovely string quartet
transcription are the ornaments. Weitzmann gives a
helpful editorial footnote as to how they should be
played. A lively tempo will bring this work to an effec-

tive conclusion.
> Length: 58 measures
> Technique: ornaments, scales, sustained and
> moving notes, finger facility

MINUET, A Major   Advancing Elementary
(from String Quartet Hob.III:60/3)

WEITZMANN, Fritz: Haydn—Easiest Piano Pieces
(Peters No. 5004).

Two-note slurs and repeated notes could be effectively introduced by this delightful little Minuet. The flavor will be enhanced by careful articulations and dynamics. Paired with another Haydn dance, this would be a good recital piece.
> Tempo: Moderato
> Length: 26 measures
> Technique: 2-note slurs, repeated notes

ALLEGRETTO, F Major   Early Intermediate
(from String Quartet Hob.III:68/4)
> (originally in D Major)

INTERNATIONAL LIBRARY OF PIANO MUSIC, Vol. 3,
Pg. 306 (University Soc.).
RICHTER, Ada: Great Piano Music, Vol. 3 (Presser).

As this composition is based on fast sixteenth-notes in the right hand and an eighth-note counterpoint in the left, it is an excellent study in scalar passages requiring finger independence. Played at a lively tempo, it could be quite effective.

> Length: 33 measures
> Technique: scales, passage work

ADAGIO, E Major   <u>Early Advanced</u>
(from String Quartet Hob.III:74/2)

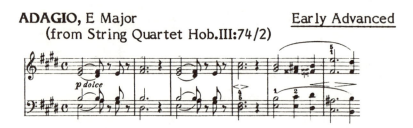

BRIMHALL, John: My First Book of Classics--Haydn
    (Hansen) theme only.
ECKSTEIN, Maxwell: Sonatina Album (C. Fischer)
    theme only.
KOHLER and KLEA: Sonatina Album
    (G. Schirmer, Vol. 51).
KOHLER and RUTHARDT: Sonatinen Album, Band F
    (Peters nr. 1233a).

This beautiful piece is considerably more difficult than it looks. Many of the figurations are tricky, both rhythmically and technically. For example, towards the end of the piece there is a 10 note (on one beat) thirty-second note flourish made up of scalar and arpeggiated figures. Isolating difficult passages for intense work will be helpful. This <u>Adagio</u> would be excellent for performance.

> Length: 64 measures
> Technique: fast runs, double notes, arpeggios,
>   scales, pianissimo control, voicing, many
>   rhythmic complexities

VARIATIONS EN RONDEAU, <u>Advancing Intermediate</u>
D Major (from Divertimento Hob.X:2/3,
"Div. a 8to stromenti")

WEITZMAN, Fritz: Dances and Pieces for the Piano
(Peters).

This charming contrapuntal piece is deceptively
difficult. The variations feature sixteenth note figurations and attractive harmonic progressions. Played at a
relaxed tempo, this piece would be quite enjoyable as a
recital selection.
> Tempo: Allegro
> Length: 88 measures
> Technique: trill-like figures, leaps, scales,
> broken 3rds

MINUET AND TRIO, C Major, <u>Advancing Elementary</u>
(from Divertimento Hob.XIV:4/4, "Divertimento con
2 Violini e Basso")

ANTHONY, George W.: Easy Bach to Kabalevsky...
(Presser).
FERGUSON, Howard: A Keyboard Anthology, Second
Series, Book Two (Belwin-Mills).
INTERNATIONAL LIBRARY OF PIANO MUSIC, Vol. 3,
Pg. 378 (University Soc.).

This elegantly refined piece is a wonderful introduction to the grace and style of the classical period. It

is simple, beautiful, and accessible. The only technical difficulties are the ornaments, and Ferguson gives some helpful and pianistic suggestions as to how they should be realized. This <u>Minuet</u> is definitely recommended for performance.

> Tempo: Tempo di Minuetto
> Length: 48 measures
> Technique: ornaments, broken 6ths and
>   octaves, scalar passages

GYPSY RONDO, G Major,   <u>Advancing Intermediate</u>
(from Trio Hob.XV:25/3)

ALFRED (Publisher): Haydn--15 of his Most Popular...
BRIMHALL, John: My First Book of Classics--Haydn
    (Hansen-H704).
HANSEN (Publisher): Joseph Haydn--A Highlight
    Collection...
MARWICK and NAGY: Creative Keyboard, Level 3
    (Columbia).
SHEALY, Alexander: Haydn--His Greatest Piano Solos
    (Ashley).
THOMPSON, John: John Thompson's Modern Course,
    Second Grade Book (Willis).

Once learned, this difficult work is quite satisfying. Some of the more technically demanding sections are omitted in various editions, giving the elementary pianist an opportunity to enjoy the piece. The Alfred and Shealy editions are complete, while the Marwick edition is slightly shortened and simplified. Brimhall, Hansen, and Thompson include only the theme.
    The rondo theme is made up of broken thirds, which are excellent for finger independence. Scales, octaves (both broken and simultaneous), arpeggios, and trills are

other technical hurdles the pianist must master.   This
piece is useful for exploring possibilities with articulations and dynamics.

> Tempo: Presto
> Length: 192 measures
> Technique: double notes (3rds and octaves),
>   broken intervals (3rds and octaves), scales,
>   trills, arpeggios, sustained and moving notes

THE HEAVENS ARE TELLING <u>Intermediate</u>
(from the Oratorio Hob.XXI:2, "The Creation")

ALFRED (Publisher): Haydn--15 of his Most Popular...

This transcription doesn't do justice to the original
beautiful choral work, and for this reason is not recommended for performance.   However, it is excellent for
developing sight reading skills.

> Tempo: Allegro
> Length: 81 measures
> Technique: sustained and moving notes,
>   chords, scales, octaves (broken and
>   double notes)

TWELVE EASY PIECES

Note: These pieces are complete in the following books:

KALMUS #3524: Joseph Haydn--12 Easy Pieces
   (Belwin-Mills).
PALMER, Willard: Haydn--12 Short Piano Pieces
   (Alfred).
PETERS (Publisher): Haydn--Short Pieces (Nr. 1120).
PHILIPP, Isadore: Joseph Haydn--Douze Petites Pieces
   (Durand Nr. 11603).

Other sources are listed with each composition.

No. 1, **ANDANTE GRAZIOSO,**   Early Intermediate
Bb Major, (from String Quartet, Hob.III:75/2)

CASTLE, Joseph: Mel Bay's Student Piano Classics--
   Haydn (Mel Bay-63069).
ECKSTEIN, Maxwell: Sonatina Album (C. Fischer).
HERRMANN, Kurt (Kalmus #9544): Easy Handel and
   Haydn (Belwin-Mills).
KALMUS #3523: A First Haydn Book (Belwin-Mills).
KOHLER, Louis: Sonatina Album, Vol. 51 (G. Schirmer).
KOHLER and RUTHARDT: Sonatinen Album, Band I
   (Peters nr. 1233a).
MIROVITCH, Alfred: Early Classics for Piano
   (G. Schirmer).
ZEITLIN and GOLDBERGER: The Solo Book IV
   (Consolidated)

   Both melodic and harmonic interest is captured in
this elegant and sentimental <u>Andante,</u> which requires
careful voicing. Some of the dotted rhythms at this
slow tempo may be tricky.

Length: 24 measures
Technique: double 3rds, sustained and moving
     notes, dotted rhythms

No. 2, **ALLEGRO,** F Major, or   <u>Advancing Elementary</u>
"Finale," "Allegro Scherzando," (from String
     Quartet, Hob.III:75/4)

AARON, Michael: Michael Aaron Piano Course,
     Grade Three (Belwin-Mills).
AGAY, Denes: Intermediate Classics to Moderns,
     Vol. 37 (Consolidated).
BASTIEN, James: Piano Literature, Vol. 3 (GWM).
BRADLEY, Richard: Bradley's Level Six Classics
     (Bradley).
BRIMHALL, John: My First Book of Classics--Haydn
     (Hansen-H704).
BRISMAN, Heskel: Classical Classics--32 All-Time
     Hits...(Alfred).
CURTIS, Helen: Fundamental Piano Series, Book 3
     (Lyon-Healy).
ECKSTEIN, Maxwell: Sonatina Album (C. Fischer).
ETTS, May L.: Beginning to Play Haydn
     (Schroeder & Gunther).
HERRMANN, Kurt (Kalmus #9544): Easy Handel and
     Haydn (Belwin-Mills).
KALMUS #3523: A First Haydn Book (Belwin-Mills).
KOHLER, KLEA, et al: Sonatina Album
     (G. Schirmer, Vol 51).
KOHLER and RUTHARDT: Sonatinen Album, Band I
     (Peters nr. 1233a).
KREUTZER, Hilde B.: 42 Favorites for Piano, Book 3
     (Brodt).
La MAGRA, Anthony: Master Repertoire...Level III,
     Vol. I (Columbia).

LANNING, Russell: Music by the Masters
(Musicord/Belwin-Mills).
McGRAW, Cameron: Four Centuries of Keyboard Music,
Book 3 (Boston).
MIROVITCH, Alfred: Early Classics for Piano
(G. Schirmer).
MOTCHANE, Marthe Morhange: An Introduction to
Pianistic Styles, Book 2, Classical (Bourne).
NEVIN, Mark: Piano Masterpieces for the Young,
Vol. One (Willis).
OLSON, BIANCHI, BLICKENSTAFF: Repertoire 5A
(C. Fischer).
PACE, Robert: Music for Piano, Book 5
(Roberts/Schirmer).
RICHTER, Ada: Great Piano Music, Vol. 4 (Presser).
ROYAL CONSERVATORY OF MUSIC, Grade 5
(Frederick Harris).
ZEITLIN and GOLDBERGER: F.J. Haydn--A Digest of
Short Piano Works (Boston-13789).

Many sudden dynamic contrasts and syncopations
enliven this light and gay work. The leaps and double
notes are the only technical problems. This <u>Allegro</u> will
give the elementary pianist an opportunity to work on
articulation. Once mastered, it is fun to play and would
go very well on a recital program.

    Length: 44 measures
    Technique: double notes, chords, octaves,
      leaps, scalar figures

No. 3, **ANDANTE,** C Major   Intermediate
(from Symphony Hob.I:94/2, "Surprise")

ALFRED (Publisher): Haydn--15 of his Easiest...
ALFRED (Publisher): Haydn--15 of his Most Popular...

BRISMAN, Heskel: Classical Classics--32 All-Time
  Hits...(Alfred).
ETTS, May L.: Beginning to Play Haydn
  (Schroeder & Gunther).
HANSEN (Publisher): Joseph Haydn--A Highlight
  Collection...
HERRMANN, Kurt (Kalmus #9544): Easy Handel and
  Haydn (Belwin-Mills).
KALMUS #3523: A First Haydn Book (Belwin-Mills).
KOHLER, Louis: Sonatina Album, Vol. 51 (G. Schirmer).
KOHLER and RUTHARDT: Sonatinen Album, Band I
  (Peters nr. 1233a).

This amusing standard transcription from Haydn's
"Surprise" Symphony presents pianistic difficulties. The
problems include double thirds in scalar passages, large
reaches, repeated notes, fast scales, and tricky
rhythms. There are also many simplified arrangements
of "Papa Haydn's" mischievious work available. This
piece would be amusing to play on a recital.
  Length: 41 measures
  Touches: legato, staccato
  Technique: double 3rds in 16th notes, large
    reaches, octaves, 16th note sextuplets,
    repeated notes, scales, chords

No. 4, **PRESTO, MA NON**   Advancing Elementary
  TROPPO, D Major (from Symphony Hob.I:93/4)

HERRMANN, Kurt (Kalmus #9544): Easy Handel and
  Haydn (Belwin-Mills).
MOTCHANE, Marthe Morhange: An Introduction to
  Pianistic Styles, Book 2, Classical (Bourne).

This transcription is quite pianistic, with easily surmounted technical difficulties. The Palmer and Kalmus editions provide suggested realizations of Haydn's ornaments.

> Length: 32 measures
> Technique: octaves, pentachords, double 3rds

No. 5, **ADAGIO CANTABILE,**   Early Intermediate
D Major (from Symphony Hob.I:92/2)

BRISMAN, Heskel: Classical Classics--32 All-Time
    Hits...(Alfred).
ETTS, May L.: Beginning to Play Haydn
    (Schroeder & Gunther).
PALMER and LETHCO: Creating Music Recital Book 5
    (Alfred).

The pianist who is technically proficient but needs work on musicality would benefit from this Adagio. Careful direction should be given to each voice. The slow tempo facilitates the technical aspects. Challenging rhythms and accidentals make this a good sight reading exercise for the more advanced student.

> Length: 21 measures
> Technique: scales, double 3rds, octaves,
>   sustained and moving notes, demanding
>   rhythms

No. 6, **VIVACE,** D Major,   <u>Early Intermediate</u>
   or "Joyful" (Hob.I:92/4)

BRISMAN, Heskel: Classical Classics--32 All-Time
   Hits...(Alfred).
CASTLE, Joseph: Mel Bay's Student Piano Classics--
   Haydn (Mel Bay-63069).
KREUTZER, Hilde B.: 42 Favorites for the Piano,
   Book 2 (Brodt).
MARWICK and NAGY: Creative Keyboard, Level 3
   (Columbia).
MIROVITCH, Alfred: Early Classics for Piano
   (G. Schirmer).
NAHUM, WOLFFE, KOSAKOFF: Piano Classics
   (C. Fischer).
ZEITLIN and GOLDBERGER: F.J. Haydn--A Digest of
   Short Piano Works (Boston-13789).

The main technical difficulty in this sprightly and
enjoyable piece is the constant broken intervals in an
alternating two-note slur, two-note staccato pattern.
Careful attention to dynamics will add verve.   This
transcription would be good on a recital if paired with a
slower piece.
          Length: 38 measures
          Technique: arpeggios, occasional double notes,
             crisp touch

No. 7, **ALLEGRO,** C Major,   Advancing Elementary
or "Allegro non Troppo," "German Dance"
(from Symphony Hob.I:95/4)

HERRMANN, Kurt (Kalmus #9544): Easy Handel and
    Haydn (Belwin-Mills).
ZEITLIN and GOLDBERGER: F.J. Haydn--A Digest of
    Short Piano Works (Boston-13789).

This charming piece is an excellent example of
Haydn's good-natured wit. It is sure to be enjoyed by
the elementary pianist as the only difficulty is fitting
the ornaments within the beat. To convey the appropriate spirit, it should be played in cut-time.
        Length: 32 measures
        Technique: double 3rds, ornaments,
            sustained and moving notes

No. 8, **ANDANTINO,** Eb Major,   Advancing Elementary
or "Rondo" (from Symphony Hob.I:85/2 "La Reine")

AGAY, Denes: Easy Classics to Moderns, Vol. 17
    (Consolidated).
ALFRED (Publisher): Haydn--15 of his Easiest...
ANTHONY, George W.: Byrd to Beethoven, Vol. I
    (Presser).
BIG-3 (Publisher): 79 Renowned Classics, Home Library
    Series, Vol. 10.

BRISMAN, Heskel: Classical Classics--32 All-Time
    Hits...(Alfred).
ETTS, May L.: Beginning to Play Haydn
    (Schroeder & Gunther).
GRANT, Lawrence: Piano Music by the Great Masters
    (Ashley).
KALMUS #3523: A First Haydn Book (Belwin-Mills).
MOTCHANE, Marthe Morhange: An Introduction to
    Pianistic Styles, Book 2, Classical (Bourne).
WEITZMAN, Fritz: Haydn--Easiest Piano Pieces
    (Peters No. 5004).
ZEITLIN and GOLDBERGER: F.J. Haydn--A Digest of
    Short Piano Works (Boston-13789).

Elegance and quaint charm characterize this lovely
Andantino. The broken interval accompaniment figure
should be subdued. This beautiful piece is very satisfying for both performer and listener.
            Tempo: Andantino, un poco allegretto
            Length: 32 measures
            Technique: double 3rds, broken intervals,
                grace notes

No. 9, **MENUETTO AND TRIO,**   Early Intermediate
    D Major (from Symphony Hob.I:92/2)

BRISMAN, Heskel: Classical Classics--32 All-Time
    Hits...(Alfred).
HERRMANN, Kurt (Kalmus #9544): Easy Handel and
    Haydn (Belwin-Mills).

Abundant contrast marks this lively and dynamic
piece, which would be enhanced by creative articula-

tion. Several instances of octaves and octave chords might be difficult for small hands. Contrapuntal lines should be emphasized in this accessible and enjoyable piece.

> Tempo: Commodo
> Length: 84 measures
> Technique: scales, chords, octaves, broken
>   3rds, double 3rds and 6ths, sustained
>   and moving notes, ornaments

No. 10, **MINUET AND TRIO,** F Major   Intermediate
   (from Symphony Hob.I:89/3)

KALMUS #3523: A First Haydn Book (Belwin-Mills).

This brilliant Minuet is contrasted with a more lyrical Trio. The Minuet requires hand independence, using two simultaneous articulations. This vital and engaging work would make a successful recital piece.

> Tempo: Allegretto
> Length: 68 measures
> Technique: double 3rds, scales, arpeggios, hand
>   independence for contrasting touches,
>   octaves

No. 11, **VIVACE ASSAI,** F Major or   Intermediate
   "Allegro, "Allegro Giocoso" (from Symphony
   Hob.I:89/4)

AGAY, Denes: Intermediate Classics to Moderns,
  Vol. 37 (Consolidated).
BRADLEY, Richard: Bradley's Level Five Classics
  (Bradley).
HERRMANN, Kurt (Kalmus #9544): Easy Handel and
  Haydn (Belwin-Mills).
MIROVITCH, Alfred: Early Classics for Piano
  (G. Schirmer).

The biggest obstacle in this fast and vivacious piece
is subduing the sixteenth-note Alberti bass. The double
thirds are not difficult, but the work demands subtle
nuance, varied articulations, and dynamic variety.
Quite familiar, this delightful piece is recommended for
recital.
  Length: 68 measures
  Technique: Alberti bass, double notes, scales

No. 12, **ANDANTE CON MOTO,** C Major   <u>Intermediate</u>
  (from Symphony Hob.I:89/2)

HERRMANN, Kurt (Kalmus #9544): Easy Handel and
  Haydn (Belwin-Mills).
ZEITLIN and GOLDBERGER: F.J. Haydn--A Digest of
  Short Piano Works (Boston-13789).
ZEITLIN and GOLDBERGER: The Solo Book IV
  (Consolidated).

This flowing piece is a useful exercise in double
notes--thirds, sixths, and octaves. Dotted rhythms and
numerous articulation changes prevail. Imaginative
dynamics will add interest.
  Length: 31 measures
  Technique: double 3rds, double 6ths,
      sustained and moving notes, octaves

V. WORKS OF DOUBTFUL OR UNKNOWN ORIGIN

In an effort to capitalize on Haydn's international popularity during the decades surrounding his death, many unscrupulous publishers issued spurious works under the master's name. These outright forgeries, combined with numerous misattributions, have formed a large body of pieces bearing Haydn's name, but are in no way connected with actual, verifiable works by the composer. Haydn's vast output has until recently defied cataloguing, and Hoboken's pioneering study accepts many works whose authenticity has not been established, or has in many cases been disproved. The problem of attribution is compounded by the numerous piano transcriptions of lost orchestral works of dubious origin. Like Haydn's own transcriptions, they are generally in small dance forms.

In spite of the problematical origins of these works, many reveal typical classical features characteristic of both Haydn and the general musical climate of the era. The delightful Oschenmenuet Hob.IX:27 derives from a lost vaudeville (c. 1805) "Le menuet du beouf, ou Une Lecon d'Haydn" by J.B. Constantine. The equally attractive German Dances Hob.IX:10 are anonymous arrangements of melodies from "L'arbore di Diana," an opera by Vicente Martin y Soler (1754-1806). Both of these works are at least as eloquent as the best of Haydn's own transcriptions. The Minuets Hob.IX:20 contain some material probably by Haydn, but the origin of most of the music is obscure.

The elimination of these pieces from the canon of authentic works by Haydn should not conceal the high quality of many of them. Though not profound, these compositions gracefully fulfill their roles as amusing and entertaining trifles. Galant charm and finely crafted elegance are found in these little pieces, many of which are suited to performance by pianists of modest ability. The pedagogical value of these works is well known, and many of them would serve as an excellent introduction to the classical style. An appreciation of these anonymous compositions is based not on the

the reputation of a famous and much loved composer, but rather on inherent musical value.

ST. ANTHONY'S CHORALE,   Advancing Elementary
Bb Major, Hob.II:46*/2

ALFRED (Publisher): Haydn--15 of his Easiest...
ALFRED (Publisher): Haydn--15 of his Most Popular...

This familiar, beautiful piece is quite accessible and enjoyable. It is excellent practice in playing and voicing chorale music. The performer should be able to hear every contrapuntal line. The slow tempo should obviate technical problems. Brahms used this melody for his famous composition, "Variations on a Theme by Haydn." This work is certainly not by Haydn, and is often attributed to Ignaz Joseph Pleyel (1757-1831).

> Tempo: Andante moderato
> Length: 29 measures
> Technique: sustained and moving notes,
>   double notes

SERENATA, C Major,   Advancing Elementary
(from String Quartet Hob. III:17/2)

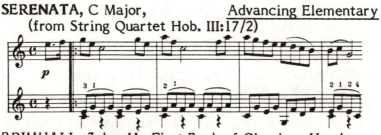

BRIMHALL, John: My First Book of Classics--Haydn
    (Hansen-H704).
ETTS, May L.: Beginning to Play Haydn
    (Schroeder & Gunther).

HANSEN (Publisher): Joseph Haydn--A Highlight
    Collection...

Long attributed to Haydn, this transcription is from
a string quartet by Roman Hoffstetter (1742-1815).
However, because of its familiarity and compositional
beauty, it is an interesting and engaging piece to play.
Brimhall and Hansen include only the theme, but the
Etts edition contains the entire movement. Because of
the technical simplicity, it provides an excellent
opportunity for the pianist to work on musical
interpretation.
> Tempo: Andante cantabile
> Length: 66 measures
> Technique: sustained and moving notes,
>   Alberti bass, appoggiaturas, turns

IX deutche Tänze (12 German Dances)
    Hob.IX:10, 1-12 (1793)

GERMAN DANCE, G Major, Advancing Elementary
Hob.IX:10/2, or "Allemande"

BRIMHALL, John: My First Book of Classics--Haydn
    (Hansen-H704).
HANSEN (Publisher): Joseph Haydn--A Highlight
    Collection...
WEITZMANN, Fritz: Haydn--Easiest Piano Pieces
    (Peters No. 5004).

The main obstacle in this lively German Dance is
the melody in double thirds. Deft phrasing is crucial in
the second section.   The Brimhall and Hansen editions
have phrasing that highlights the linear aspects of the
piece. The sustained and moving notes in the left hand

may be a problem for the pianist with small hands.
>Tempo: no indication
>Length: 24 measures
>Technique: double 3rds, sustained and moving
> notes

GERMAN DANCE, C Major,   Advancing Elementary
>Hob.IX:10/3

ANSON, George: Survey of Piano Literature, Level 1,
>Book 1--Early Keyboard Music (Elkan-Vogel).
BRIMHALL, John: My First Book of Classics--Haydn
>(Hansen-H704).
HANSEN (Publisher): Joseph Haydn--A Highlight
>Collection...

This joyful <u>German Dance</u> provides an excellent opportunity for experimentation with dynamics. The second section may pose problems because of the broken octaves in the left hand and the melody in double sixths in the right. Several of these German dances would make enjoyable recital selections.
>Length: 16 measures
>Technique: broken octaves, double 6ths

GERMAN DANCE, F Major,   Advancing Elementary
>Hob.IX:10/4

BRIMHALL, John: My First Book of Classics--Haydn
    (Hansen-H704).
ETTS, May L.: Beginning to Play Haydn
    (Schroeder & Gunther).
HANSEN (Publisher): Joseph Haydn--A Highlight
    Collection...

Although the first section of this German Dance is
harmonically mundane, it has melodic charm.   Con-
versely, the second section is melodically repetitive, but
the harmonies are unusual. Yet, on the whole, the piece
is delightful and enjoyable.
> Length: 16 measures
> Technique: L.H. octaves

GERMAN DANCE, Bb Major,   Advancing Elementary
    Hob.IX:10/5

HEINRICHSHOFEN (Publisher): Haydn--Easier
    Favorites, Urtext (Peters No.4049).

Lovely   melodies,   demanding   careful   phrasing,
characterize this German Dance. With the exception of
several "sf" markings, dynamics are left to the discre-
tion of the performer. The Alberti bass figures should
be subdued.
> Length: 16 measures
> Technique: LH sustained and moving notes,
>   Alberti bass

GERMAN DANCE, Eb Major,   <u>Advancing Elementary</u>
   Hob.IX:10/6

ANSON, George: Anson Introduces Haydn--German
   Dances (Willis-9962).
ETTS, May L.: Beginning to Play Haydn
   (Schroeder & Gunther).
HEINRICHSHOFEN (Publisher): Haydn--Easier
   Favorites, Urtext (Peters No.4049).

   Quick grace notes in the regular phrase structure
lend charm to this short dance. The second section
contains important accents. Heinrichshofen suggests
that this be performed as the <u>Trio</u> of the preceding
<u>German Dance Hob.IX:10/5.</u>
      Length: 16 measures
      Technique: 3rds in left hand, grace notes,
         scalar passage

GERMAN DANCE, E Major,   <u>Advancing Elementary</u>
   Hob.IX:10/8 or "Allemande"

ANSON, George: Anson Introduces Haydn--German
   Dances (Willis-9962).
HEINRICHSHOFEN (Publisher): Haydn--Easier
   Favorites, Urtext (Peters No.4049).
WEITZMANN, Fritz: Haydn--Easiest Piano Pieces
   (Peters No. 5004).

This engaging dance is fun to play and delightful to hear.   The left hand Alberti bass figure and the right hand scalar melodic figure must be carefully synchronized.   The unison melody in the second section creates a welcome tonal digression from the tonic key. Repetition of phrases makes this an excellent selection for ease of memorization.

>Tempo: Allegro (in Anson)
>Length: 16 measures
>Technique: scales, Alberti bass

GERMAN DANCE, A Major,   Advancing Elementary
   Hob.IX:10/9

HEINRICHSHOFEN (Publisher): Haydn--Easier
   Favorites, Urtext (Peters No.4049).

This German Dance is technically easy and could be assigned to an elementary level student who can reach an octave. The one instance of double thirds should not be a problem. In this edition the piece functions as the Trio of No.IX:10/8.

>Length: 16 measures
>Technique: scales, double 3rds, octave leaps

Menuetti (18 Minuets with 7 Trios and an Aria)
   Hob.IX:20, 1-18 (date unknown)

MINUET, A Major, Hob.IX:20/13 Advancing Elementary

ZEITLIN and GOLDBERGER: The Solo Book II
(Consolidated).

An occasional octave leap is the only technical
aspect of this charming piece which prevents it from
being on the elementary level. Otherwise, it is easily
accessible. There are many unison passages, though
occasionally the left hand will have either a counter-
melody or an accompanimental figure. Efficient fingering is needed in the scalar passages. The terraced
dynamics should be slightly exaggerated.
>Tempo: Moderato
>Length: 20 measures
>Technique: scalar passages

MINUET, D Major, Hob.IX:20/15   <u>Advancing Elementary</u>

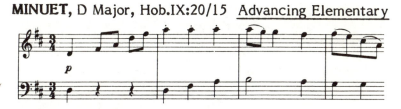

ZEITLIN and GOLDBERGER, The Solo Book II
(Consolidated).

This piece sounds easier than it actually is. Although much of it is rather awkward, it is good for work
on arpeggios and cross-over fingerings. The melodies
are charming. Once the technical obstacles are overcome, the performer should emphasize the various
articulations and phrasings which characterize the
playful nature of this <u>Minuet</u>.
>Tempo: Allegretto
>Length: 18 measures
>Technique: arpeggios, octaves, careful
>   fingering

Ballo tedescho (10 deuthche Tänze) (10 German Dances)
Hob.IX:22,1-10 (date unknown)

GERMAN DANCE, D Major,   <u>Advancing Elementary</u>
Hob.IX:22/1

AGAY, Denes: Easy Classics to Moderns, Vol. 17
(Consolidated).
BRADLEY, Richard: Bradley's Level Four Classics
(Bradley).
BRADLEY, Richard: Easy Teaching Pieces...Vol. 2
(Bradley).
KALMUS #3525: Joseph Haydn--10 German Dances
(Belwin-Mills).
WEYBRIGHT, June: Belwin Piano Method, Book 5
(Belwin-Mills) (with coda from Hob.IX:22/10).

This ever-popular dance is fun to play and not
technically demanding. The left hand must be subdued
in the second section. Otherwise, no serious problems
surface in this fine recital piece.
Tempo: Allegretto
Length: 16 measures
Technique: octaves, scalar passages

GERMAN DANCE, D Major,   <u>Elementary</u>
Hob.IX:22/2 or "Minuet," "Country Dance,"
"Peasant Dance," "Dance"

ACKERMAN, Gloria: Piano Guide for First Year
  Students (Belwin-Mills).
AGAY, Denes: Easy Classics to Moderns, Vol. 17
  (Consolidated).
AGAY, Denes: From Bach to Bartok, Vol. A (Warner).
AMSCO (Publisher): It's Easy to Play Classics.
BASTIEN, James: Easy Piano Classics (Kjos West).
BASTIEN, James: First Piano Repertoire Album
  (Kjos West).
BASTIEN, James and Jane: Beginning Piano for Adults
  (Kjos West).
BASTIEN, James and Jane: Piano Second Time Around
  (Kjos West).
BRADLEY, Richard: Bradley's Level Four Classics
  (Bradley).
BRADLEY, Richard: Easy Teaching Pieces...Vol. 2
  (Bradley).
BRISMAN, Heskel: Classical Classics--32 All-Time
  Hits...(Alfred).
ETTS, May L.: Beginning to Play Haydn
  (Schroeder & Gunther).
GLOVER, David Carr: Piano Repertoire, Level Six
  (Belwin-Mills).
GRANT, Lawrence: Piano Music by the Great Masters
  (Ashley).
KALMUS #3525: Joseph Haydn--10 German Dances
  (Belwin-Mills)
KREUTZER, Hilde B.: 42 Favorites for Piano, Book I
  (Brodt).
McGRAW, Cameron: Four Centuries of Keyboard Music,
  Book I (Boston)
NEVIN, Mark: Piano Course, Book 3 (Belwin-Mills).
NEVIN, Mark: Piano Masterpieces for the Young,
  Vol. One (Willis).
OLSON, BIANCHI, BLICKENSTAFF: Repertoire 4A
  (C. Fischer).
OZANIAN, Carole: Piano Album, Level 1a (Studio P/R).

Unison staccato notes (hands two octaves apart)
begin this march-like piece. Careful fingering is
required, and the chords in the left hand in the second

half of the work should be subdued. This pleasant and accessible work is fine for a recital if paired with another German dance.

>Tempo: Allegretto
>Length: 16 measures
>Technique: grace notes

GERMAN DANCE, G Major,   Advancing Elementary
Hob.IX:22/3

AGAY, Denes: Easy Classics to Moderns, Vol. 17
    (Consolidated).
ALFRED (Publisher): Haydn--15 of his Easiest...
BRADLEY, Richard: Bradley's Level Four Classics
    (Bradley).
BRADLEY, Richard: Easy Teaching Pieces...Vol. 2
    (Bradley).
FERGUSON, Howard: A Keyboard Anthology, Book I,
    First Series (Associated Board).
GRANT, Lawrence: Piano Music by the Great Masters
    (Ashley).
KALMUS #3523: A First Haydn Book (Belwin-Mills).
KALMUS #3525: Joseph Haydn—10 German Dances
    (Belwin Mills)
WELCH, John: Schroeder's First Recital (Studio P/R).

Each hand has its own melody in this delightful dance. Various editions might be consulted for different ideas on articulation.

>Tempo: Andantino
>Length: 16 measures
>Technique: hand independence

GERMAN DANCE, Eb Major, Hob.IX:22/4   <u>Elementary</u>

ANSON, George: Anson Introduces Haydn--German
   Dances (Willis).
KALMUS #3523: A First Haydn Book (Belwin-Mills).
KALMUS #3525: Joseph Haydn--10 German Dances
   (Belwin-Mills)
PACE, Robert: Music for Piano, Book 4
   (Roberts/Schirmer).

   This prosaic piece might be useful as an introduction to phrasing. It is harmonically straightforward and
technically easy.
         Tempo: Allegretto
         Length: 16 measures
         Technique: triads

GERMAN DANCE, Bb Major,   <u>Advancing Elementary</u>
   Hob.IX:22/5, or "Country Dance," "Minuet"

AGAY, Denes: Easy Classics to Moderns, Vol. 17
   (Consolidated).
BRADLEY, Richard: Bradley's Level Four Classics
   (Bradley).
BRADLEY, Richard: Easy Teaching Pieces...Vol. 2
   (Bradley).
GRANT, Lawrence: Piano Music by the Great Masters
   (Ashley).
KALMUS #3525: Joseph Haydn--10 German Dances
   (Belwin-Mills)

SHEALY, Alexander: Haydn--His Greatest Piano Solos
(Ashley) F Major.

The only stumbling block in this pleasant dance is
the dotted rhythm found in beats 2 and 3 involving the
"short-long" or "Scotch Snap" (♪♩.). The constant left
hand accompaniment must be subdued.   The two-note
phrases will be facilitated by a relaxed wrist.
Tempo: Moderato
Length: 16 measures
Technique: scalar passages

GERMAN DANCE, G Major,   Advancing Elementary
Hob.IX:22/6

KALMUS #3523: A First Haydn Book (Belwin-Mills).
KALMUS #3525: Joseph Haydn—10 German Dances
(Belwin-Mills)
NOONA, Walter and Carol: The Classical Performer 3
(Heritage).

The only major technical hurdle is in the last four
measures where the right hand has the melody and the
left hand has an Alberti bass figure.   Both the melody
and the accompaniment in this dance are static and
rather dull, and if it is performed, dynamics must be
exaggerated to propel the piece forward.
Tempo: Allegro
Length: 16 measures
Technique: scalar passages, sustained bass
note and accompanying intervals

GERMAN DANCE, D Major, Hob.IX:22/7   <u>Elementary</u>

AGAY, Denes: Easy Classics to Moderns, Vol. 17
  (Consolidated).
ALFRED (Publisher): Haydn--15 of his Easiest...
BRADLEY, Richard: Bradley's Level Four Classics
  (Bradley).
BRADLEY, Richard: Easy Teaching Pieces...Vol. 2
  (Bradley).
GRANT, Lawrence: Piano Music by the Great Masters
  (Ashley).
KALMUS #3523: A First Haydn Book (Belwin-Mills).
KALMUS #3525: Joseph Haydn--10 German Dances
  (Belwin-Mills)
NOVIK, Ylda: Young Pianist's Guide to Haydn
  (Studio P/R).
WELCH, John: Schroeder's Favorite Classics, Vol. I
  (Studio P/R).

Tone production can be effectively developed in this charming dance. The left hand broken chord accompaniment needs control to bring out the parallel tenth melody and to subdue the "thumpy thumb." The phrasing differs among editions, and Novik gives some pedalling indications. Double thirds and broken octaves in the second half are not difficult at a moderate tempo. The piece is quite accessible and suitable for performance.

  Tempo: Allegretto
  Length: 16 measures
  Technique: broken octaves, double 3rds

GERMAN DANCE, A Major,   <u>Advancing Elementary</u>
Hob.IX:22/8

ALFRED (Publisher): Haydn--15 of his Easiest...
KALMUS #3523: A First Haydn Book (Belwin-Mills).
KALMUS #3525: Joseph Haydn--10 German Dances
    (Belwin-Mills)

This blithe and sprightly dance will be most effective if a single pulse per measure is felt. No major
technical difficulties occur, though the pianist with
small hands may have trouble with the octave chords. A
flexible wrist is needed for the two-note slurs.
        Length: 16 measures
        Technique: double notes (3rds and 6ths),
            sustained and moving notes

GERMAN DANCE, E Major,   <u>Advancing Elementary</u>
Hob.IX:22/9, or "Country Dance," "Minuet"

AGAY, Denes: Easy Classics to Moderns, Vol. 17
    (Consolidated).
BRADLEY, Richard: Bradley's Level Four Classics
    (Bradley).
BRADLEY, Richard: Easy Teaching Pieces...Vol. 2
    (Bradley).
CLARK and GOSS: Piano Literature...Book 2
    (Summy-Birchard) F Major.
GRANT, Lawrence: Piano Music by the Great Masters
    (Ashley).

KALMUS #3523: A First Haydn Book (Belwin-Mills).
KALMUS #3525: Joseph Haydn--10 German Dances
(Belwin-Mills)
McGRAW, Cameron: Four Centuries of Keyboard
Music..Book I (Boston) F Major.
NOONA, Walter and Carol: The Classical Performer 3
(Heritage).
NOVIK, Ylda: Young Pianist's Guide to Haydn
(Studio P/R).
OLSON, BIANCHI, BLICKENSTAFF: Repertoire 3B
(C. Fischer).

This dance begins in a declamatory unison, hands
two octaves apart. Creative articulation should be used
to propel this section. Care should be taken not to
begin this piece too quickly.
Tempo: Allegro
Length: 16 measures
Technique: scalar passages

GERMAN DANCE, A Major,   Advancing Elementary
Hob.IX:22/10

AGAY, Denes: Easy Classics to Moderns, Vol. 17
(Consolidated).
AGAY, Denes: An Anthology...The Classical, Vol. II
(Yorktown) no coda.
BARRATT, Carol: Chester's Piano Book No. Five
(Chester) no coda.
BRADLEY, Richard: Bradley's Level Four Classics
(Bradley) no coda.
BRADLEY, Richard: Easy Teaching Pieces...Vol. 2
(Bradley).

GRANT, Lawrence: Piano Music by the Great Masters
   (Ashley) no coda.
KALMUS #3525: Joseph Haydn--10 German Dances
   (Belwin-Mills)

   Melodic charm characterizes this <u>German Dance</u>. It
is useful as both an introduction to double notes in a
combination of touches and phrasings, and as an exercise in tone production. The left hand is of secondary
importance throughout, functioning mainly as accompaniment. The playful character of this dance will be
enhanced if a single pulse per measure is felt.
   Tempo: Moderato
   Length: 16 measures (coda - 24 measures)
   Technique: double notes (3rds)
NOTE: a coda based on material from the first German
Dance Hob.IX:22/1 concludes the set.

<u>Minuet</u> Hob.IX:24 (Connected with Hob.IX:29)
   (date unknown)

MINUET, C Major, Hob.IX:24   <u>Elementary</u>

BRADLEY, Richard: Big Note Teaching Pieces...Vol. I
   (Bradley).
CLARK and GOSS: Piano Literature...Book 2
   (Summy-Birchard).
OLSON, BIANCHI, BLICKENSTAFF: Repertoire 3B
   (C. Fischer).
RICHTER, Ada: Great Piano Music, Vol. I (Presser).
SCHOLZ, Erwin Christian: Music for the Home--
   Joseph Haydn (includes Quadrille Hob.IX:29/6,
   and the Trio for Hob.IX:24)

   Elegance and stateliness characterize this dance.

There are no technical problems, and the pianist should concentrate on dynamics, articulations, and the two independent contrapuntal lines. Care should be taken to play the triplets and ornaments exactly in time. Easily memorized, this piece is excellent for performance.

> Tempo: Andante
> Length: 16 measures
> Technique: turns

Ochsenmenuett (Oxen-Minuet) Hob.IX:27 (c.1805)

MINUET AND TRIO, C Major, Hob.IX:27,   Intermediate
  "Oxen Minuet"

CASTLE, Joseph: Mel Bay's Student Piano Classics--
  Haydn (Mel Bay-63069).
SHEALY, Alexander: Haydn--His Greatest Piano Solos
  (Ashley).

This Minuet is rhythmically, harmonically, and pianistically intriguing. It is excellent for developing left hand independence. The double thirds in the left hand, the octaves in the right hand, and the entire trio are omitted in the easier Castle edition (advancing elementary). A very lively piece, it provides excellent opportunities for creative dynamics and articulations. This Minuet would be a fine performance selection.

> Tempo: Moderato
> Length: 38 measures
> Technique: double octaves, 3rds, and 6ths,
>   broken 3rds, scales, sustained and moving
>   notes, various touches, repeated notes

<u>Zingarese</u> (8 Gypsy Dances) Hob.IX:28/1-8 (1799)

GYPSY DANCE (Zingarese),   <u>Advancing Elementary</u>
   C Major, Hob.IX:28/1

AGAY, Denes: The Joy of Classics (Yorktown).
ZEITLIN and GOLDBERGER: F.J. Haydn--A Digest of
   Short Piano Works (Boston-13789).
<u>Trio only:</u>
AGAY, Denes: More Easy Classics to Moderns, Vol. 27
   (Consolidated).
BRADLEY, Richard: Bradley's Level Four Classics
   (Bradley).
BRADLEY, Richard: Easy Teaching Pieces...Vol. 2
   (Bradley).
ETTS, May L.: Beginning to Play Haydn
   (Schroeder & Gunther).
GRANT, Lawrence: Piano Music by the Great Masters
   (Ashley).
OLSON, BIANCHI, BLICKENSTAFF: Repertoire 3B
   (C. Fischer).

   The A section of this <u>Gypsy Dance</u> has a pleasant
melody but suffers from a monotonous blocked chordal
accompaniment.
   The <u>Trio</u> (in AABA form) appears in many editions
by itself, and is lively and highly accessible. The contrasting B section includes a temporary change of
harmony and some piquant syncopations.
         Tempo: Allegro
         Length: 32 measures (Trio-16 measures)
         Technique: scalar figures, syncopation

GYPSY DANCE (Zingarese)   <u>Advancing Elementary</u>
F Major, Hob.IX:28/2

ZEITLIN and GOLDBERGER: F.J. Haydn--A Digest of
Short Piano Works (Boston-13789).

Valuable as an etude, this <u>Gypsy Dance</u> has little
musical content. It is extremely dull harmonically, and
the scalar passages lack direction. The double thirds in
the right hand in the <u>Trio</u> may also pose a problem.
  Tempo: Vivace
  Length: 32 measures
  Technique: scales, double 3rds, large leaps,
    syncopation

GYPSY DANCE (Zingarese)   <u>Advancing Elementary</u>
D Minor, Hob.IX:28/6

NOONA, Walter and Carol: The Classical Performer 4
(Heritage).

Harmonically, this piece is extremely interesting.
Right hand finger facility is required for the constant
sixteenth note runs. A downward leap of an octave
after a brief thirty-second note passage in the last
measure may prove a problem. Once mastered, this
work would be effective in performance.
  Tempo: Allegro molto
  Length: 16 measures
  Technique: 16th note scalar runs, octave leap

GYPSY DANCE (Zingarese) D Minor,   <u>Intermediate</u>
   Hob.IX:28/8

SCHOLZ, Erwin Christian: Music for the Home With
   Joseph Haydn (Bosworth).

Interesting and exotic sounds permeate this unusual
<u>Gypsy Dance</u>, making it enjoyable and accessible.
However, as with the other Gypsy dances, the harmonic
language and accompanimental figuration is strange and
repetitive.   The fluid tonality begins in A minor, progresses through G minor and concludes with a Picardy 3rd
in D minor. The accompaniment consists of solid chords
which never change figuration.
         Tempo: Poco allegro
         Length: 16 measures
         Technique: scalar figures, repeated notes,
            appoggiaturas, accidentals

<u>Contredanze</u> (5 Contradanses with Quadrille and Minuet
   Hob.IX:29, 1-6, date unknown)

CONTREDANSE, F Major,   <u>Advancing Elementary</u>
   Hob.IX:29/1

CLARK and GOSS: Piano Literature...Book 3
   (Summy-Birchard).
ZEITLIN and GOLDBERGER: F.J. Haydn--A Digest of
   Short Piano Works (Boston-13789).

This lively and joyful dance is in an ABC form. The outer two sections are fun and playable, but the middle one is made up of sixteenth note double thirds that are difficult at the prescribed tempo. With the necessary wrist flexibility in the B section, this Contredanse would be an exciting recital piece.

> Tempo: Allegretto (con brio)
> Length: 24 measures
> Technique: double 3rds, broken octaves

CONTREDANSE, Bb Major,   Advancing Elementary
     Hob.IX:29/2

ZEITLIN and GOLDBERGER: F.J. Haydn--A Digest of
     Short Piano Works (Boston-13789).

Rhythm presents the only problem in this jolly piece. The first section is made up of ♩ ♩♩ and the second section has ♪♪♪ figures. It may prove difficult at first to alternate between duple and triple beat divisions, but the piece is not technically taxing and is enjoyable to play.

> Tempo: Allegro
> Length: 16 measures
> Technique: scalar figures

CONTREDANSE, C Major,   Early Intermediate
     Hob.IX:29/3

ZEITLIN and GOLDBERGER: The Solo Book III
(Consolidated).

Like many other contredanses, this one is characterized by a sprightly mood, three part structure, and a
more difficult middle section. In this dance the middle
section contains double thirds in sixteenth notes. Slow
practice with a relaxed wrist and careful fingering will
be helpful. Paired with another contredanse, this would
be good for performance.

Tempo: Allegretto
Length: 24 measures
Technique: scalar double 3rds, scales

CONTREDANSE, G Major, <u>Advancing Elementary</u>
Hob.IX:29/4

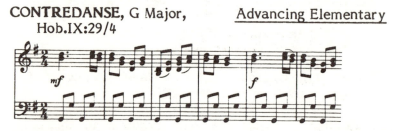

ZEITLIN and GOLDBERGER: F.J. Haydn--A Digest of
Short Piano Works (Boston-13789).

The left hand broken octaves in the first section of
this joyful piece should be subdued. Though a good
exercise in double note two-note slurs, it may be a bit
difficult at first. A loose wrist and careful fingering
should solve the problem. Performed with other
Contredanses, this work would make a good recital
selection.

Tempo: Allegretto
Length: 16 measures
Technique: double notes, ornaments, broken
octaves

CONTREDANSE, Eb Major, Hob. IX: 29/5

Advancing Elementary

ZEITLIN and GOLDBERGER: F.J. Haydn--A Digest of Short Piano Works (Boston-13789).

This interesting piece starts softly (mp), and each subsequent section becomes a little louder until the last forte in this effective edition. Each section is also a variation of the first. It is fun to play and full of charm and wit.

Tempo: Andantino
Length: 24 measures
Technique: double notes, broken octaves,
2 against 3

QUADRILLE, C Major, Hob.IX:29/6

Advancing Elementary

CLARK and GOSS: Piano Literature...Book 2 (Summy-Birchard).
SCHOLZ, Erwin Christian: Music for the Home With Joseph Haydn (Bosworth).

The double thirds in the melody are the only technical problem, yet can be readily mastered at the given tempo. This piece would be quite satisfying for the less experienced pianist as it is interesting and festive without being overly difficult. Scholz has a Menuetto and Trio (Hob.IX:24) in addition.

Tempo: Con Brio
Length: 32 measures
Technique: double 3rds

ARIA, F Major, Hob.XVII:F1   <u>Advancing Elementary</u>

ALFRED (Publisher): Haydn--15 of His Easiest...

A beautiful and expressive elegance is found in this simple Adagio. The charming melody and counter-melody provide an excellent introduction to phrasing. The most difficult aspects are the triplet arpeggios in the left hand and one appoggiatura. At a slower tempo these difficulties can be easily mastered.

Tempo: Andante molto moderato
Length: 18 measures
Technique: triplet arpeggios, simple double
    notes

WORKS WITHOUT HOBOKEN CATALOGUE NUMBERS

ALBUM LEAF, A Major   <u>Early Intermediate</u>

ALFRED (Publisher): Haydn--15 of his Most Popular...
SHEALY, Alexander: Haydn--His Greatest Piano Solos
    (Ashley).

This expressive piece requires musicality and careful voicing and shaping of the inner lines. The

technical problems can be easily overcome at this
leisurely tempo.
> Tempo: Moderato
> Length: 39 measures
> Technique: scales, sustained and moving notes,
>   double 3rds, arpeggios, broken octaves

ALLEGRETTO, C Major   <u>Advancing Elementary</u>

ROYAL CONSERVATORY OF MUSIC, Grade III
    (Frederick Harris).
SZAVAI-VESPREMI: Album for Piano, No. 2
    (Musica Budapest/Belwin-Mills).

Employing a variety of different articulations, this
charming piece must be played with spirit. Two contrapuntal lines should be heightened throughout. Scalar
figures and easy broken thirds occur. A brisk tempo
would enhance the liveliness of this fine <u>Allegretto</u>.
> Tempo: Grazioso
> Length: 46 measures
> Technique: broken 3rds, scales, sustained and
>   moving notes

GERMAN DANCE, G Major   <u>Elementary</u>

AGAY, Denes: The Joy of Recital Time (Yorktown).

In the style of a Landler, this effective <u>German Dance</u> is charming and vivacious. Broken interval two-note slurs will challenge the beginning pianist.
Tempo: Allegretto
Length: 20 measures
Technique: sustained and moving notes

MINUET AND TRIO, Bb Major   <u>Early Intermediate</u>

ZEITLIN and GOLDBERGER: F. J. Haydn--A Digest of
Short Piano Works (Boston).

This beautiful work belong not in the classical period but rather in the galant--almost late baroque. Stately elegance, harmonic variety, and dotted rhythms provide the grace and interest which make it a fine piece to play. The triplet figures in the right hand with melodic figures in the left may cause a problem of entangled hands. Clarity of line is essential.
Tempo: Moderato
Length: 71 measures
Technique: octave reaches, ornaments, simple
    arpeggios broken between the hands

MINUET AND TRIO, C Major   <u>Advancing Elementary</u>

ZEITLIN and GOLDBERGER: F.J. Haydn--A Digest of
Short Piano Works (Boston-13789).

This stately Minuet and Trio is full of classical poise
and grace. Musically, the Trio is slightly more successful than the Minuet. The ornaments may prove tricky,
and the listed edition contains no editorial suggestions.
Performance is recommended.
> Tempo: Allegretto
> Length: 76 measures
> Technique: ornaments, simple scales

MINUET AND TRIO, F Major   <u>Early Intermediate</u>

ZEITLIN and GOLDBERGER: F.J. Haydn--A Digest of
Short Piano Works (Boston-13789).

This Minuet and Trio is an example of the galant
style at its most imaginative. An occasional instance of
two against three and various ornaments are the only
trouble spots. The performer can experiment with
articulations and dynamics in this pleasing recital
selection.
> Tempo: Andantino
> Length: 48 measures
> Technique: ornaments, simple arpeggios,
>   scalar figures

MINUET AND TRIO, G Major   <u>Advancing Elementary</u>

SCHWERDTNER, Hans-G.: Easy Piano Pieces and
Sonatinas (Schott).

Schwerdtner gives helpful suggestions on playing the
ornaments in this accessible and enjoyable piece. The
difficulties include a broken octave pattern in the left
hand, double thirds, and triplets following eighth notes.
To add interest, the pianist should be as creative as
possible with articulations and dynamics.

Length: 46 measures
Technique: ornaments, broken octaves,
    double notes, scalar passages

ROMANCE, D Major   <u>Elementary</u>

ETTS, May L.: Beginning to Play Haydn
(Schroeder & Gunther).

The only hindrance in this pretty and playable piece
is the left hand leap of a tenth in the second to the last
measure. The beautiful melody will make a good exercise in phrasing. The left hand should be subdued
throughout.

Tempo: Andante
Length: 16 measures
Technique: slow Alberti bass, double notes,
    large leap

VI. WORKS FOR MUSICAL CLOCK ("Flötenuhr")

The eighteenth century had a profound fascination for all types of automatons and mechanical devices. This passion for automated gadgetry, itself a manifestation of the age's espousal of scientific rationalism and the mechanistic world-view, inspired many of the finest musicians of the era to compose works for a variety of machine-driven musical instruments. Among these, the musical clock (flötenuhr) had the greatest range and expressive potential, and composers as eminent as Mozart and Haydn created substantial works in this appealing and distinctive medium.

The term "musical clock" is something of a misnomer, as the title is applied to instruments of a particular type, some of which are supplied with chronometers and others that are not. The voice of the musical clock is the product of a system made up of a pair of bellows, a pinned cylinder, tuned pipes, and a spring or weight-driven clockwork mechanism. When set in motion, the clockwork drives the rotating cylinder, which activates the bellows. The pins of the cylinder are also linked to a device that triggers the appropriate pipes, thus producing the distinct and incisive tone of the instrument. The musical clock is essentially a small mechanical organ, and its characteristic sound in no way resembles the modern "music box." The musical clock exploits a range of up to three octaves, with F below middle C as its lowest note. It is possible to create quite complex music on the instrument, and this great artificial virtuosity combined with the unique, penetrating tonal quality drew Haydn to the musical clock.

Three mechanical instruments survive for which Haydn provided the musical material. All three were built by the Esterhazy court librarian, Father Primitivas Niemecz, a friend and former pupil of the composer. The clocks are dated 1772, 1792, and 1793, though it has been suggested that the first instrument was actually built at about the same time as its companions. Still in working order, these instruments give a fairly accurate impression of Haydn's musical style, yet the ravages of time and worn mechanisms have taken their toll, rendering the clocks inadequate testaments to true eighteenth century performance practices.

Haydn's compositions for musical clock include both original pieces and a number of virtually recomposed transcriptions of movements from his larger works. The aesthetic of the day held the art of transcription in high esteem and these arrangements should be regarded as musically authentic. The composer's personal acceptance of transcription should be taken into account when considering the innumerable arrangements by other hands of Haydn's music.

Much of Haydn's work is of an occasional nature, intended for a single performance, and as a result contains desultory passages and inconsistencies. However, the pieces for musical clock were obviously subject to constant repetition, inducing Haydn to produce finely honed works of great subtlety and imaginative variety.

Many of these delightful miniatures are very effective on the modern piano, and indeed Haydn may have had Hob. XIX:27 published in a piano version in 1794. Though brief, the pieces are technically challenging due to the mechanical facility of the musical clock, and a performance at the piano requires dexterous coordination and well-developed technique. A wide range of character and affect is explored and will test the pianist's musical sensitivity. A selection of several of these tiny masterpieces would be immensely entertaining on recital programs, and many of these works would serve as brilliant and effective encores.

WORKS FOR MUSICAL CLOCK: CONTENTS AND SOURCES (Listed in order of Schmid Publication)

1792:
#1. Hob.XIX:17
#2. Hob.XIX:10
#3. Hob.XIX:18

#4. Hob.XIX:19...from song "Warnung an ein Mädchen,"
    Hob.XXVIa:13
#5. Hob.XIX:20...from Symphony "La Reine,"
    Hob.I:85/3 (trio)
#6. Hob.XIX:8
#7. Hob.XIX:21
#8. Hob.XIX:7
#9. Hob.XIX:22
#10. Hob.XIX:23...from Symphony Hob.I:C6/4
    also attributed to Dittersdorf
#11. Hob.XIX:9...from quartet Op. 54 #2 Hob.III:57/3
#12. Hob.XIX:24

1772:
#13. Hob.XIX:1...from aria "La raggazza col vecchione"
    from the opera "Il Monda della Luna" Hob.XXVIII:7
#14. Hob.XIX:2
#15. Hob.XIX:3...from Symphony "L'Imperiale"
    Hob.I:53/2
#16. Hob.XIX:4...melody by Giornovichi, later used by
    Beethoven for Variations on a Russian Theme
#17. Hob.XIX:5...from Trio Hob.XI:82/3
#18. Hob.XIX:6...from Trio Hob.XI:76/3
(The 1772 clock contains the following pieces in the
    Schmid collection: #'s 23, 22, 13-15, 21, 16, 20, 19,
    8, 6, 17, 11, 18, 2, and 24)

1793:
#19. Hob.XIX:11
#20. Hob.XIX:12
#21. Hob.XIX:13
#22. Hob.XIX:14
#23. Hob.XIX:15
#24. Hob.XIX:16
#25. Hob.XIX:25...from Military March Hob.VII:6
    previously attributed to Beethoven
#26. Hob.XIX:26...attributed to Schuster
#27. Hob.XIX:27...published in piano version by
    Artaria in 1794.
#28. Hob.XIX:28...from Quartet Op. 71#1 Hob. III:70/4

#29. Hob.XIX:29...from Symphony "Clock" Hob.I:101/3
#30. Hob.XIX:30...from Quartet "Lark" Op.64#5
    Hob.III:63/4

WORKS SURVIVING IN MANUSCRIPT ONLY
#31. Hob.XIX:31
#32. Hob.XIX:32...from Symphony Hob.I:99/4)

Note: #'s 4, 5, 7, 9, and 10 are not preserved in
    manuscript. Transcriptions have been made from
    the instrument by Ernst Fritz Schmid.

Note: All of the musical clock pieces are found in
    the following publication:

SCHMID, Ernst Fritz: Werke für das Laufwerk
    (Flötenuhr) or Works for Musical Clock for Piano
    Solos (Nagel #802).

Other sources are listed with each composition.

No. 1 **ALLEGRO MODERATO,**   Advancing Intermediate
    C Major, Hob.XIX:17

        An abundance of clever and charming figuration
marks this piece. A brisk steady tempo is needed.
            Length: 40 measures
            Technique: Alberti bass figurations,
                ornaments, arpeggios, double notes,
                scales, cadenza-like runs

No. 2 **ANDANTE,** C Major   <u>Advancing Intermediate</u>
    Hob.XIX:10

Galant style and charm are exemplified by this lovely piece. A little pedal on the arpeggiated grace notes will produce an effect close to that of the musical clock. Following the few articulations and experimenting with dynamics will reveal the engaging qualities of this <u>Andante</u>.

      Length: 18 measures

      Technique: arpeggios, scales, ornaments

No. 3 **PRESTO,** C Major   <u>Advancing Intermediate</u>
    Hob.XIX:18

Although the musical clock was incapable of dynamic nuance, the piano provides rich opportunities for echo effects and swells. Either a Presto or Allegro moderato tempo works well. Haydn's famous sense of humor is evident, especially in measures 17-19.

      Length: 50 measures

      Technique: broken chord figurations,
        ornaments,scales, double 3rds

No. 4 **ANDANTE,** C Major Hob.XIX:19   <u>Intermediate</u>

Unlike some of the other musical clock pieces, this one is delightfully pianistic. The contrapuntal lines should be distinct. Creative dynamics will bring out the simple and dignified character of this piece.

>Length: 34 measures
>Technique: scales, ornaments, 32nd notes,
>   double notes

No. 5 C Major, or   <u>Advancing Elementary</u>
  "Minuet, "Musical Box" Hob.XIX:20

WATERMAN and HAREWOOD: The Young Pianist's
  Repertoire (Faber).

In transcribing this unusual piece for piano, much of the novelty has been lost. It is harmonically and melodically dull, relying on the unique sound of the musical clock for its interest. Fingerings should be carefully planned.

>Length: 34 measures
>Technique: double 3rds, arpeggios

No. 6 **MINUET,** C Major or "Der <u>Intermediate</u>
Wachtelschlag" (Call of the Quail) Hob.XIX:8

Many aspects of this minuet are more idiomatic to
the musical clock than the piano, yet these difficulties
are readily overcome. For example, in the three-voiced
passage toward the end the middle voice could more
easily be taken by the left hand. However, "Der
Wachtelschlag" is delightful and well worth the effort.

> Length: 20 measures
> Technique: arpeggios, repeated notes, double
> notes, ornaments, scales, sustained and
> moving notes

No. 7 **ALLEGRETTO,** C Major Hob.XIX:21 <u>Intermediate</u>

This quite unusual piece starts with a relatively
short passage in G major, and concludes with a lengthier
section in C. The performer should bring as much verve
as possible to this joyful piece. Careful fingering and
slow practice help to facilitate the many double thirds.
This charming miniature should be played with great
enthusiasm.

> Length: 48 measures
> Technique: double 3rds

No. 8 **MINUET**, C Major, Hob.XIX:7   <u>Intermediate</u>

This stately <u>Minuet</u> is characterized by an abundance of static dotted rhythms. The constant double notes are quite playable at this tempo. The arpeggiated cadenza-like figures provide a welcome and refreshing change from the repetitive character of the other sections.

          Length: 26 measures
          Technique: double 3rds and 6ths, arpeggios,
               sustained and moving notes

No. 9 **ALLEGRO MODERATO**,   <u>Advancing Intermediate</u>
    C Major, Hob.XIX:22

This extraordinarily appealing piece is slightly awkward but great fun to learn and play. The many double notes and rolled chords with acciaccaturas are just two of the quirks which give this work such an original flavor. This delightful piece would make an appropriate encore for the more experienced pianist.

          Length: 30 measures
          Technique: double 3rds, sustained and moving
               notes, rolled chords, scalar figures,
               ornaments

No. 10 **VIVACE,** C Major   <u>Advancing Intermediate</u>
Hob.XIX:23

    Vivacious and charming with abundant fast runs and difficult contrapuntal lines, this longer piece is definitely worth the effort it requires. The pianist should meticulously observe the notated articulations, and strive for clarity in the scale passages.
          Length: 40 measures
          Technique: scales, broken octaves, double
            notes, ornaments, rolled chords

No. 11 **MINUET,** C Major Hob.XIX:9   <u>Intermediate</u>

ALFRED (Publisher): Haydn--15 of his Easiest...
ALFRED (Publisher): Haydn—15 of his Most Popular...
FERGUSON, Howard: Oxford Keyboard Classics--Haydn
    (Oxford).

    The lively nature of this <u>Minuet</u> will be accentuated if the articulations are carefully observed. Subtle dynamic nuance will enhance the piece. The extended trills should be subdued and played lightly and clearly.
          Tempo: Allegretto
          Length: 24 measures
          Technique: double notes, trills in both hands,
            broken chords, scales

No. 12 **PRESTO,** C Major   Advancing Intermediate
      Hob.XIX:24

This exuberant piece should be played with spirit and enthusiasm. The slightly awkward and less pianistic sections require rhythmic stability. A brisk tempo with dynamic contrast will heighten the fun and gaiety.

> Length: 50 measures
> Technique: broken chords, trills, broken and
>   double 3rds, broken 6ths and octaves,
>   arpeggios, scales

No. 13 **ALLEGRETTO,** F Major   Advancing Intermediate
      Hob.XIX:1

An idiomatic clock sound replete with rolled chords and acciaccaturas permeates this engaging piece. Played with proper spirit and enthusiasm, a delightful effect can be achieved. This unique and lovely piece would work well either as part of a set, or by itself as an encore.

> Length: 26 measures
> Technique: scales, rolled chords, ornaments,
>   arpeggios, broken chords

No. 14 **VIVACE**, F Major Hob.XIX:2   <u>Early Advanced</u>

A jolly and happy piece, this work exemplifies Haydn's famous sense of humor and good-natured disposition. Unfortunately, the scalar double thirds could prevent it from being played with the carefree abandon it requires. Slow practice with meticulous attention to fingering should help alleviate this problem.

Length: 35 measures

Technique: grace notes, scales, scalar double
3rds, broken intervals, sustained and
moving notes

No. 15 **ANDANTINO,** F Major   <u>Early Advanced</u>
Hob.XIX:3

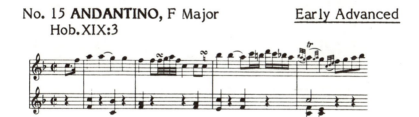

This engaging piece is structurally simple but somewhat unpianistic. Careful fingering will alleviate this problem. Several difficult trills can be modified or omitted.

Length: 24 measures

Technique: ornaments, sustained and moving
notes, double notes, chromatic scale, trills

No. 16 ANDANTE CANTABILE   Early Advanced
(Der Dudelsack, The Bagpipe) C Major, Hob.XIX:4

In this piece, Haydn effectively captures the hypnotic charm of 18th century peasant music. The harmonies are often static but lovely melodies occur throughout. Both performer and audience should enjoy "Der Dudelsack."

> Length: 42 measures
> Technique: double notes, broken intervals,
>   ornaments, scalar figures

No. 17 **MINUET,** F Major   Advancing Elementary
Hob.XIX:5

WATERMAN and HAREWOOD: The Young Pianist's
    Repertoire (Faber).

Simpler and more accessible than most, this Minuet contains some of Haydn's subtle humorous interjections. It is more pianistic than many of the musical clock pieces.

> Length: 28 measures
> Technique: double 3rds, octave reach

No. 18 **VIVACE,** F Major   <u>Intermediate</u>
(Der Kaffeeklatsch) Hob.XIX:6

Haydn's subtitle "Der Kaffeeklatsch" helps the performer to capture the spirit of this piece. To bring out the effect of people gossiping and drinking coffee, this scherzo should be played with a happy and bouncy feel. It would make a wonderful encore.

> Length: 40 measures
> Technique: scales, repeated notes, double
>   notes

No. 19 **ALLEGRETTO,** C Major Hob.XIX:11   <u>Advanced</u>

This brilliant and evocative work contains many awkward passages which make it difficult to convey the appropriate carefree spirit. Once mastered it would be an excellent recital selection when grouped with others, or a convincing encore.

> Length: 36 measures
> Technique: quick ornaments, rolled chords,
>   chromatic and diatonic scales and runs,
>   broken chords and arpeggios, scalar double
>   3rds, 32nd notes

No. 20 **ANDANTE**, C Major Hob.XIX:12   Advanced

Even at an Andante tempo this work is still incredibly difficult for the piano, with an extended trill and scalar line together in one hand which is virtually impossible to play. However, it is a beautiful piece and the trill could be omitted.

Length: 24 measures
Technique: rolled chords, ornaments, scales,
    broken chords, double notes, broken interval
    figuration, sustained and moving notes

No. 21 **VIVACE**, C Major Hob.XIX:13   Advanced

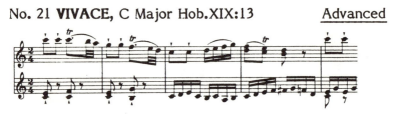

Fast and exuberant, this difficult piece is more pianistic than many of its companions. The most problematic aspect is the double sixth passage. The scalar passages require verve and bravura. This piece would work well in performance.

Length: 48 measures
Technique: ornaments, scales, broken interval
    figurations, double notes, broken chords

No. 22 **MINUET**, C Major Hob.XIX:14   Early Advanced

This sprightly work is effective on the modern piano. Good finger facility is needed for the cadenza-like arpeggios and characteristic runs. Clarity and style should be goals in performance.

Length: 36 measures

Technique: double notes, ornaments, scales, arpeggios, chords, chromatic scale, sustained and moving notes

No. 23 ALLEGRO MA NON TROPPO, C Major, Hob.XIX:15

Although difficult, this delightful and engaging work will reward the effort expended on it. The tempo must be fast but not frantic, with an exuberant and spirited sound. This wonderful piece is well suited for performance purposes.

Length: 49 measures

Technique: broken chords, broken intervals, double notes, rolled chords, ornaments, scales, repeated notes, scalar figures

No. 24 FUGA, C Major Hob.XIX:16

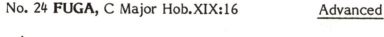

This intricate fugue (the only one in the set) contains a number of pianistic difficulties. The double thirds and contrapuntal lines are the chief technical problems. Clear voicing is essential. The work is an excellent study in fugal style.

Tempo: Allegro
Length: 39 measures
Technique: ornaments, double 3rds, sustained
    and moving notes, scales, rolled chords

No. 25 **MARCHE**, D Major Hob.XIX:25   Early Advanced

A unique quality characterizes this piece. Although rhythmically vital it is not bombastic, sounding more like a march for children or toy soldiers. The typical musical clock sound that pervades this piece is wonderfully jolly and gay. This march would provide a festive conclusion to a recital.

Tempo: Marche
Length: 30 measures
Technique: scales, double notes, repeated
    notes and chords, ornaments, complex
    rhythms

No. 26 **ANDANTE - ALLEGRO,** E Major   Advanced
    Hob.XIX:26

<u>Andante:</u> Although unique because of its two-movement form, this piece falls short of the calibre of some of the others. Yet it is still charming and intriguing. The rhythms and figurations are complex.

Length: 20 measures
Technique: scales, ornaments, grace notes,
    acciaccaturas

Allegro: The most difficult aspect of this movement is the eccentric and confusing rhythm. A steady pulse will accentuate the grotesque character of this unusual Polonaise.

> Length: 16 measures
> Technique: sustained and moving notes, scalar
>   figures, broken intervals, repeated notes,
>   broken chords, erratic rhythms, 32nd notes

No. 27 **ALLEGRETTO**, G Major Hob.XIX:27   Advanced

This beautiful piece is one of the most mature, complete, and fully developed of the set. It possesses a kind of delicate clarity which only a sensitive pianist can express. The difficult and unpianistic passages consist of both a trill and another voice, often in double notes, occuring in the same hand. To facilitate matters, it would be appropriate to omit the trill in these passages if one is to perform this work with the style and ease its idiom suggests.

> Length: 35 measures
> Technique: ornaments, repeated notes, rolled
>   chords, chromatic and diatonic scale
>   figures, broken chords, double notes,
>   sustained and moving notes, broken intervals

No. 28 ALLEGRO, C Major Hob.XIX:28   <u>Advanced</u>

Haydn's good-natured sense of wit and spirit are exemplified by this bouncy, at times almost teasing work. Though pianistic, difficulties arise in grace notes and scalar double notes and chords. The piece should flow along at a quick and lively tempo.

> Length: 57 measures
> Technique: grace notes, double notes, octaves,
>   sustained and moving notes, broken interval
>   figuration, broken and rolled chords, scales

No. 29 MINUET, C Major   <u>Advancing Intermediate</u>
Hob.XIX:29

Accessible as well as beautiful, this piece is quite pianistic and poses no insurmountable problems. It is stately and galant, and the beat should be kept as steady as possible when executing the ornaments.

> Length: 80 measures
> Technique: double 3rds, ornaments, scalar
>   figures, broken intervals

No. 30 PRESTO, G Major Hob.XIX:30   <u>Advanced</u>

This brilliant and flamboyant work requires bravura. There are a few awkward passages such as the scalar double thirds in the left hand, but most of these problems can be solved with correct and thoughtful fingering. This jovial <u>Presto</u> may be effedtively grouped with the previous three, Nos. 27, 28, and 29. These four played together sound like a short sonata. Excellent performance material, these four pieces are unique and exciting.

> Length: 64 measures
> Technique: scales, broken chords, double
> notes, sustained and moving notes, rolled
> chords, repeated notes, broken intervals

No. 31, **ALLEGRETTO,** C Major Hob.XIX:31 <u>Advanced</u>

Though musically delightful, this piece is awkward and unpianistic. It possess an idiomatic and attractive clock-like sound. The pianistic problems may be mitigated by a slower tempo.

> Tempo: Allegretto
> Length: 38 measures
> Technique: scales, ornaments, double 3rds,
> broken chords, rolled chords, difficult
> hand-crossing

No. 32 **ALLEGRO,** F Major, Hob.XIX:32 <u>Advanced</u>

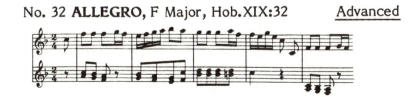

This is one of the most enjoyable pieces in the entire set. Except for the passage (typical of these pieces) in which there is an extended trill and another voice in double notes all in one hand, this Allegro is well-suited to the piano. The difficult trill could be omitted.

Length: 96 measures
Technique: scales, double notes, ornaments, sustained and moving notes, broken chords, arpeggios, rolled chords

BIBLIOGRAPHY

Friskin, James and Freundlich, Irwin. Music for the Piano. New York: Dover, 1973.

Gillespie, John. Five Centuries of Keyboard Music. New York: Dover, 1965.

Grout, Donald Jay. A History of Western Music. New York: Norton, 1980.

Grove, Sir George. The New Grove Dictionary of Music and Musicians. Edited by Stanley Sadie. London: Macmillan, 1980.

Hinson, Maurice. Guide to the Pianist's Repertoire. Bloomington: Indiana University Press, 1973.

Hinson, Maurice. Guide to the Pianist's Repertoire: Supplement. Bloomington: Indiana University Press, 1979.

Hoboken, Anthony van. Joseph Haydn: Thematischbibliographisches Werkverzeichnis. Mainz: B. Schott's sohne, 1957.

Kern, Alice M. and Titus, Helen M. The Teacher's Guidebook to Piano Literature. Ann Arbor: Edwards Brothers, 1964.

Kirby, F. E.. A Short History of Keyboard Music. New York: Schirmer, 1966.

Landon, H. C. Robbins. Haydn: Chronicle and Works. Vols. 1-5. Bloomington: Indiana University Press, 1980.

Landon, H. C. Robbins. Haydn: A Documentary Study. New York: Rizzoli, 1981.

Lockwood, Albert. Notes on the Literature of the Piano. Ann Arbor: University of Michigan Press, 1940.

INDEX

190 Index

INDEX BY TITLE AND KEY